MY DAD & ME

MY DAD & ME

*A Heartwarming Collection of
Stories About Fathers from a Host
of Larry's Famous Friends*

LARRY KING

 CROWN PUBLISHERS   NEW YORK

Grateful acknowledgment is made to the following for permission
to use excerpts from their previously published work:

The song lyric "My Father." Copyright © 1968 by Judy Collins.
Reprinted by permission of the Universal Music Publishing Group.

"Flash Cards," from *Grace Notes* by Rita Dove. Copyright © 1989
by Rita Dove. Used by permission of the author and W. W. Norton
& Company, Inc.

Library of Congress Cataloging-in-Publication Data
My dad and me : a heartwarming collection of stories
about fathers from a host of Larry's famous friends /
[edited by] Larry King.—1st ed.
1. Conduct of life—Miscellanea. I. King, Larry, 1933–
BJ1595.M9   2006
170'.44—dc22   2005027753

ISBN-13: 978-0-307-23653-1
ISBN-10: 0-307-23653-6

Printed in the United States of America

Design by Barbara Sturman

10 9 8 7 6 5 4 3 2 1

First Edition

With gratitude to fathers everywhere

Acknowledgments

M y sincere thanks to Dana Beck and the staff of Bill Adler Books, Jeanne Welsh, Lisa Iannucci and the staff of Adler Robin Books, Ed Randall, and Michael Patrick Shiels. Finally, this book would not have been possible without the exceptional work of William Schrom.

Contents

MY DAD & ME

Introduction by Larry King

My father died when I was nine and a half years old, but I have very distinct, strong memories of him. I think about him almost all the time. My brother, who was six and a half when our father died, has no memory of him. We had lost a brother before I was born. My father had lost a son to a burst appendix. He was five years old. So my father really took care of me. He took me to Yankee games. In fact, I smoked when I was seventeen because he smoked. He died very suddenly from a heart attack. He was only forty-seven. He came here from Austria, and I felt very close to him. I got to know my mother very well after he died. He was a patriot. He had a little business that he sold to work in a defense plant to help his country. As an adopted American, he felt intensely loyal. He was just a special kind of guy. One of the values he taught me was never to lie. In fact, once we were sitting at the dinner table and he asked me how I had liked Hebrew school that day, and I said, "Fine." He whacked me in the head, and I fell down. He had run into a kid who said I wasn't in Hebrew school that day. That was a lesson well learned.

A father provides us with some of the most important life lessons of all. He can be a friend, a disciplinarian, a nurturing parent, a seemingly endless well of experience, our greatest enemy, and our greatest hero. Oftentimes, he can be all of these things at once.

For this book, I have personally asked famous people from all walks of life to share with us, in their own words, memories, lessons, and tidbits of advice from their fathers. Although the range of experiences within this book is vast, everyone here, like the rest of us, is moved by that unique and special influence of his or her father.

I have had the unique opportunity to interview thousands of people during my career, and the importance of fatherhood and the passing on of knowledge and experience has always been a truly powerful topic. This book contains offerings from social leaders, entertainers, writers, athletes, and other successful people, all of whom are tied together by their appreciation for the dynamic and rewarding task of fatherhood.

I believe you will find their words insightful and enjoyable, funny at times, poignant at others, and always celebratory of the wonderful gift of fatherhood.

Chinua Achebe

A prolific novelist, an editor, and an educator, Chinua Achebe has won countless awards for his vital contributions to African and English literature. His novel Things Fall Apart *has sold more than 10 million copies all over the world and is considered by many one of the hundred greatest novels ever written. He is currently a professor of languages and literature at Bard College.*

My father was born in the 1880s when English missionaries were first arriving among his Igbo people. He was an early convert and a good student, and by 1904 was deemed to have received enough education to be employed as a teacher and an evangelist in the Anglican mission.

The missionaries' rhetoric of change and newness resonated so deeply with my father that he called his first son Frank Okwuofu (New Word). The world had been tough on my father. His mother had died in her second childbirth, and his father, Achebe, a refugee from a bitter civil war in his original hometown, did not long survive his wife. My father therefore was not raised by his parents (neither of whom he remembered) but by his maternal uncle, Udoh. It was this man, as fate would have it, who received in his compound the first party of missionaries in his town. The story is told of how Udoh, a very generous and tolerant man, it seemed, finally asked his visitors to move to a public playground on account of their singing, which he considered too dismal for a living man's compound. But he did not discourage his young nephew from associating with the singers.

The relationship between my father and his old uncle was instructive to me. There was something deep and mystical about it, judging from the reverence I saw and felt in my father's voice and demeanor whenever he spoke about his uncle. One day in his last years he told me a strange dream he had recently had. His uncle, like a traveler from afar, had broken a long journey for a brief moment to inquire how things were and to admire his nephew's "modern" house of whitewashed mud walls and corrugated iron roof.

My father was a man of few words, and I have always regretted that I did not ask him more questions. But I realize also that he took pains to tell me what he thought I needed to know. He told me, for instance, in a rather oblique way of his one tentative attempt long ago to convert his uncle. It must have been in my father's youthful, heady, proselytizing days! His uncle said no, and pointed to the awesome row of insignia of his three titles. "What shall I do to these?" he asked my father. It was an awesome question. What do I do to who I am? What do I do to history?

An orphan child born into adversity, heir to commotions, barbarities, and rampant upheavals of a continent in disarray—was it at all surprising that my father would eagerly welcome the explanation and remedy proffered by diviners and interpreters of a new word?

And his uncle, a leader in his community, a moral, open-minded man, a prosperous man who had prepared such a great feast when he took the OZO title that his people gave him a praise-name for it—was he to throw all that away because some strangers from afar had said so?

Those two—my father and his uncle—formulated the dialectic that I inherited. Udoh stood fast in what he knew but he also left room for his nephew to seek other answers. The answer my father found in the Christian faith solved many problems, but by no means all.

His great gift to me was his love of education and his recognition that whether we look at one human family or we look at human society in general, growth can come only incrementally, and every generation must recognize and embrace the task it is peculiarly designed by history and by providence to perform.

From where I stand now, I can see the enormous value of my great-uncle, Udoh Osinyi, and his example of fidelity. I also salute my father, Isaiah Achebe, for the thirty-five years he served as a Christian evangelist and for all the benefits his work, and the work of others like him, brought to our people. I am a prime beneficiary of the education that the missionaries made a major component of their enterprise. My father had a lot of praise for the missionaries and their message, and so do I. But I have also learned a little more skepticism about them than my father had any need for. Does it matter, I ask myself, that centuries before European Christians sailed down to us in ships to deliver the Gospel and save us from darkness, other European Christians, also sailing in ships, delivered us to the transatlantic slave trade and unleashed darkness in our world? Just a thought.

Patch Adams, M.D.

In 1972, Dr. Patch Adams founded the Gesundheit! Institute, an organization based on promoting available and compassionate health care throughout America and the world. A physician, a social activist, a performer, and an author, he was the subject of a feature film starring Robin Williams in 1998.

My father died when I was sixteen as a result of war. He was a professional soldier who fought during World War II and in Korea. Before he died of body, he died in his soul and heart to me, his second of two sons. My father met my mom in New York City for a weekend furlough in the fall of 1944, and I was born on May 28, 1945. He first saw me long after I was born. Half of the sixteen years we had together, he was away being a soldier, an officer.

Today, his lost humanity would be foolishly and simplistically called post-traumatic stress syndrome. I don't hear it being said that maybe the natural, healthy response to the horror of war (even when you fight for "good") is to crumble inside, like the most potent allergic reaction (of mind) I have experienced. Healthy people cannot help but be traumatized by it. For the doctor in me, it is evidence of mental health to be traumatized by war—especially if you participated. Growing up on army bases, I saw the palpable trauma in the countless officer parties that consisted of heavy drinking and smoking. The only weeping I remember Dad doing came when he was asked about the wars. It is very natural for a son to ask questions about his father's job. As a kid, at home, when he was in Korea—every day I thought he could be killed. As I went from age six to age nine, I began to imagine what he was doing to others.

I thought he didn't love me as I grew up. I was a sissy, a nerd; he was the big athlete. As a teenager, I crumbled when he died suddenly. We had just begun to talk (he apologized for not playing with me and told me a lot of war stories). We moved to the South in

1961, gallantly engaged, fighting racism. I was shocked, horrified at the segregation and at how few people spoke up against it. I went to marches and sit-ins. I connected the spirit of hatred I felt in that struggle with what had killed my father—just another form. I did not fit in. When I was seventeen and eighteen, I was hospitalized. I hurt from the stupid horror. I wanted to die, unable to understand the adult world's choosing violence and injustice over compassion and generosity. These qualities—compassion and generosity—found pure expression in my mom.

In the last hospitalization, on a locked ward, I put my intelligence to reading and interviewing and understanding all that had happened. There were alternatives to the violence and injustice. My attempted suicide had simply joined the style. I think I became a citizen and said to myself that since I am concerned about peace and justice, then I must speak up and provide alternatives. It was a call to be proactive (a call my father answered in 1942). Inherent in the effort is the opportunity to feel fulfilled with meaning. I have found this to be one of life's enchantments.

I have lived every minute since leaving the mental hospital in 1963 in service to peace, justice, and caring for others. My father was instrumental in that choice, so indirectly my father gave me my life's work. I decided to be nonviolent, so during the Vietnam War I put great effort into getting a conscientious objector status and

8

succeeded in 1971. I was declared unfit to kill. My children also automatically earn the same status. What a gift Dad gave me to protect myself and children from harm. I am so glad I have not hurt people.

I'm sure the same ethical river, the activism I rode on, led me to create our free model hospital project and zealously stick to it all this time (it's been heaven). I quickly and clearly saw the relationship between what wars are all about and what prevents the richest country of the world from caring for all of its citizens. In the last twenty-one years, I have also led as many as nine clown trips in one year. We have taken clowns into war zones three times and into many refugee camps. It is the sweetest time of my life. My brother and both of my sons assist me in this work. Combined, they made a total of ten trips in 2004.

Dad showed me the work I must do and was smart enough to court my mom and wed her. She gave me the tools needed to carry out the work with relentless glee and creativity.

Finally, Dad was an intellectual, well read in literature and ideas. When he was home while I was growing up, I saw him, in his chair, drinking and smoking heavily while reading books. Reading has been so important to me that no other pastime has intoxicated me like it has. If his reading got me reading, then I kiss his feet.

As I reflect on all this, more than I have ever done before, I feel a well of gratitude for my life of nonviolence and working for justice for all people. I'm a happy man because I was never involved in a war. I want to thank Dad for the richness of my life in such bountiful quests every day. But I would have traded all these lessons his life gave me for a regular dad, present, playful, and tender.

Bertie Ahern, T.D.

Former Dublin mayor Bertie Ahern is the youngest prime minister in the Republic of Ireland's modern history. He assumed the post at the age of forty-five after twenty years as a member of Parliament. He was born and attended school in Dublin.

My father always said to me, "Be truthful with yourself and always be truthful with others."

You may ask how I have been in public life for more than thirty years considering the latter part of my father's advice!

My father came from a generation that put so much emphasis on personal qualities such as truth, dignity, and respect for others. He was a wise man, but, like many of his day, he did not wear his wisdom on his sleeve. He was actively involved in the struggle for Irish independence and passionately believed in the rights and freedoms that all people should enjoy. He also knew at times that there was a terrible price to pay for such rights. And I think that is why I have always sought to understand both sides of an argument, that no one is ever totally right or wrong, that respect is due to all protagonists, and that everyone needs to be heard.

He was a quiet man, devoted to my mother and his family, and although his words were sparse, I always knew he wanted me to aspire to the values he held close. They were simple values, the same as any father would instill in his children. I would like to think that they have helped me along my life's journey.

Buzz Aldrin

In 1969, Buzz Aldrin became only the second man to walk on the moon as part of the Apollo 11 crew. He founded the ShareSpace Foundation, a nonprofit organization dedicated to promoting space tourism.

M y father taught me to work very hard in school and persevere with my goals. He was an excellent example: a good Air Force pilot with a doctoral degree. I graduated near the top of my class at West Point. I got my doctoral degree at MIT. I was a decorated fighter pilot in Korea. I wanted to be an astronaut—and after being turned down the first time, I persevered and became one. I shot for the moon, and I got there.

Jayne Meadows Allen

Actress Jayne Meadows Allen has received numerous honors for her work on stage, screen, and television. She made her Broadway debut in 1941, and has worked continuously ever since, often appearing with her husband, Steve Allen.

My father, Rev. Francis J. M. Cotter, served for fourteen years as an Episcopalian missionary in the "Temple of Hell" district outside the city of Wuchang, in China, a poverty-stricken cotton-mill town on the banks of the Yangtze River. Today, Wuchang is better known as the birthplace of the Chinese Revolution. It was also my birthplace.

One stormy afternoon, while playing a game of jacks with my friend Shăo Li, son of one of my father's converts, I became so annoyed by Li's repeated cheating that I hauled off and fired a handful of metal jacks with all the power my six-year-old arm could muster, landing a bull's-eye on his nose.

Blood spurted like a faucet from poor Li's face. I don't remember who screamed the loudest, but I do recall a sobbing Li fleeing our compound, leaving me in a state of shock.

Fortunately, my father, working on his sermon in the next room, had heard enough to fear the worst. The sight of a bloodied Chinese child staggering out of an American Christian mission is all the Communist leaders would have needed to incite a riot. Talk about manna from heaven. These revolutionaries had already threatened our lives and those of the entire congregation on several occasions.

Without stopping for an umbrella, my father grasped my hand and, with the simple command "Hurry, you must find Li and apologize," we were out in the muddy streets, which were teeming with the usual weary peasants suffering their endless struggle for survival.

We discovered dear Li huddled against our massive brick wall under the Communist Executioner's Box, which neighbored our compound. An old beggar woman held his little face to the cleansing rain.

My father swept Li into his arms and rushed him back to our mission clinic. I sheepishly followed, struggling with my tearful apology.

There are times when that terrifying experience is as vivid to me as it was almost eighty years ago. Had it not been for the sensitivity of my dear father, we might all have been executed.

In fact, later that year, 1927, Generalissimo Chiang Kai-shek launched a violent purge against the Communists in Wuchang, and the first bomb in his campaign landed inside our compound. It went through our house and landed on our dining room table but never exploded.

We took the hint and escaped that night aided by several trusted parishioners, among them Shăo Li's parents.

My saintly father was one of the greatest preachers who ever graced a pulpit, but it was his example as a truly loving human being that I cherish, always.

Sparky Anderson

Hall of Famer Sparky Anderson is the only man in Major League Baseball history to lead both National and American League teams to World Series victories (the Cincinnati Reds in 1975 and 1976 and the Detroit Tigers in 1984). He was inducted into the Hall of Fame in 2000.

When I was eleven years old, my father told me, "There's one thing you can do in your lifetime that will be free and cost you nothing, and that is to be nice to people."

If every father would tell that to every one of his children, he couldn't give them a better gift. Keep the money, but give them that gift.

Piers Anthony

Piers Anthony is a prolific and bestselling author specializing in the genre of fantasy fiction. He is the author of the popular Xanth series as well as the Incarnations of Immortality books.

When I was young, my father read to me and told me stories. If there was a chore to do, such as digging a ditch, he would read a story and then paraphrase it, telling it to my sister and me as he worked, making the chore entertaining. At night, he would read to us, and this was always a favorite time. When I grew up and had children of my own, we read stories similarly, including some of the same material, such as *The Arabian Nights,* a truly grand fantasy series. Thus the legacy of reading and storytelling was passed along the generations.

So perhaps it is not surprising that I retained a strong affinity for storytelling. I was blessed or cursed with an extremely active imagination, and in adulthood was able to harness it in the form of commercial fiction. Writing was the governing force of my life and career, and I became a successful author of fantasy novels. My father's storytelling was not intended to be a lesson, but I believe it was a fine one. It certainly had a profound effect on me.

Mike Babcock

Canadian hockey coach and former player Mike Babcock coached the NHL's Anaheim Mighty Ducks from 2002 to 2005, leading the team to its first appearance in the Stanley

Cup Finals. He is now the head coach of the NHL's Detroit Red Wings.

My father, also named Mike, was in the mining industry in Saskatchewan and all across Canada. He had a very straightforward work ethic: "Never ask anybody in your life to work harder than you're willing to work." As a leader, you have to give your all every day because you want your employees—or in my case, players—to be professional and prepared. I want to be a model to my players, because it's not what I say that's important, it's what I do—and I don't want to let any coach in the league outwork me.

James Bacon

Columnist James Bacon has covered the Hollywood beat since 1948, and has also appeared in several films, including the Planet of the Apes series. As a writer, he has worked with both the Associated Press and the Los Angeles Herald-Examiner.

My father taught me to respect the other guy's feelings at all times and, above all, to be nonadversarial in dealing with people. Elizabeth Taylor once said in a TV interview that I was "unbitchy," which I took as a compliment to my father's advice. I inherited from him an easygoing nature and a don't-give-a-damn attitude toward life's obstacles.

Max Baer Jr.

Max Baer Jr. is an actor, a director, and a producer, best known for his work on The Beverly Hillbillies *television show. His father, Max Adelbert Baer, was a heavyweight boxing champion in the 1930s and a hero for many working-class people during the Depression.*

My father, Max Adelbert Baer, was born on February 11, 1909, in Omaha, Nebraska. He was the thirteenth heavyweight boxing champion of the world.

When I was seventeen, I was fairly tough and I thought I knew everything—including that "anybody" over thirty years old should be in the "old folk's home."

In the summer of 1955, my dad said to me, "You're not tough enough until you can take me!" He was in his midforties and weighed 240 pounds (I was 200 pounds).

So I said, "Okay!" With sixteen-ounce gloves, we started to box in the backyard. I was pretty fast and hit my dad with a good body punch. He grinned, lowered his head, and started to stalk me.

My mother yelled from the upstairs bedroom, "Max! Don't hurt him!" I said, "I won't," thinking she was talking to me! Just then, my dad barely touched me with a left jab. I felt nothing—like a touch of a feather.

The next thing I remember was my mother's voice coming from far, far away, screaming, "You've killed him! You've killed him!"

I was on my back on the cool grass. My eyes were open, but I couldn't see anything until my dad's face came clearly into focus. "Are you okay, son?" he asked. I don't remember what I said exactly, but my dad helped me to my feet. My legs felt like spaghetti, but I stayed upright.

What happened? My dad had hit me with a right-hand punch—I never saw it coming! What's funny is that there was no pain! I was just knocked out.

I learned some very important lessons that day. One, I wasn't so tough, and two, my dad was afraid of me. Afraid if he ever hit me again, he would kill me! He died in 1959.

I wish he were here to hit me again.

Kaye Ballard

Kaye Ballard is an actress, a singer, and a comedian who has starred in television, in film, and on Broadway in a career spanning sixty years. She got her start in show business as a vaudeville singer.

When I told my father that I wanted to go into show business, he said, "Take five or ten dollars out of every paycheck you earn. Put it in the bank. Don't touch it until you are fifty years old!" Oy . . . double oy! If only I had listened to his advice!

Bill Barber

A professional hockey forward for the Philadelphia Flyers, Bill Barber helped lead the team to two Stanley Cup championships during the mid-1970s, and his impressive playing skill landed him in the Hockey Hall of Fame in 1990. He then went on to coach the NHL's Philadelphia Flyers.

My dad had a great deal of influence over me growing up, and his life lessons still affect me to this day, even though he passed away in August 1985. He made me accountable for my actions from the time I was a small boy.

He loved the game of hockey more than a lot of kids I played with through minor hockey. We lived out in the country and had a small farm. I was one of five boys, and my father built us an outdoor rink beside the house so we could skate and play hockey with the neighboring kids.

My dad was an eccentric man of few words and always had a method to his madness. He knew that if he pushed me to the limit at a young age, I would have an opportunity to play this great game of hockey. And, like all good fathers, he was continually pushing me in the right direction. He pushed me to practice harder than I ever would have on my own. I remember him saying from the side of the rink, "Stop practicing what you're good at; practice what you find difficult." That's how I was able to skate left to right while most players only excel in one direction.

I worked with my father in my early teens and learned his work ethic and commitment to work and family. He was a generous man, but he would not make it easy for us. I resented how hard we had to work sometimes, spending a Saturday chopping wood instead of going to the lake with my friends, but after making it as a hockey player in the NHL, I appreciated why he pushed me the way he did. I never would have made it without him.

But the best lesson my father ever taught me when I was growing up was a lesson that wasn't spoken but rather taught through his example and through his actions. Terms that come to mind are "work ethic," "sacrifice," and "honesty." Those principles are the foundation on which I have built my life and the concepts that I strive to live by on a daily basis. For that, I will forever be grateful and in debt to this courageous man—my father, Harry Barber.

Joanna Barnes

Joanna Barnes has appeared in such films as Auntie Mame *and* Spartacus *and has published several novels as well as a popular syndicated column. Her books include* Pastora *and* Silverwood *and have been published worldwide.*

B oy, was my father right when he said to me: "Don't
marry anyone who cannot make you laugh!"

Senator Evan Bayh

Born in Shirkieville, Indiana, Senator Evan Bayh served as
governor of Indiana before being elected to the U.S. Senate
in 1998. His father, Senator Birch Bayh, served as senator
for Indiana from 1963 to 1981 and ran against Jimmy Carter
for the 1976 Democratic nomination for president.

W hen I was a boy, people would sometimes ask
me what it was like to have a father who was so
often in the public eye. This usually came as a surprise
to me because I never saw him as a public figure. I was
his son, and I loved him like a son. Nothing else was
relevant. He was a father first and a senator second.
Despite the demands of his job and the travel it re-
quired, my father was sometimes one of only two or
three parents at my Little League games. He was there
for me whenever I needed him, without question. To
say that I idolized my dad throughout my childhood
would not be much of an overstatement.

As I grew older, I began to understand what motivated my father to work as hard as he did. Both he and
my mother taught me that the essential thing in life
is not what you take out of it, but what you put back,

and what is important is not who helps you, but what you can do to help others. The bills my father labored over in Washington seemed far away to me, but he showed me that they could make a real difference in people's lives.

It was my admiration for my father that led me to volunteer for his political campaign when he decided to run for president in 1976. For me, the campaign was a transforming experience that taught me how exhilarating it could be to work for a cause and a candidate in whom you believe. Although I always knew that my father and I were similar in many respects, it was during those months that I learned I shared his dedication to public service.

Now, as I serve as a U.S. senator for the people of Indiana, like my father did twenty years before me, I recognize that much of what I do is shaped by my father's influence. Even though our solutions differ occasionally, we share the same values. We are both men of faith who love America, and all of our decisions come from that foundation.

For the past decade, we also have had something else of crucial importance in common—we are both fathers. When I tuck my boys into bed each night, I understand why my father rushed home to my Little League games, because now I do the same. (Although my boys, true Hoosiers that they are, are more interested in basketball than baseball.) More than anything else, the desire to be a good father is perhaps the greatest value my dad passed on to me. I'll never forget the first time I held my boys in my arms. I never wanted anything so much in my life than to do whatever I could to give my sons every opportunity possible to fulfill their God-given potential.

My experiences as a father and son have opened my eyes to an emerging social crisis. Today, 24 million children have no real relationship with their father. This growing epidemic has real consequences for our country. Children who grow up without the love and care of a father are five times more likely to live in poverty, and more likely to bring weapons and drugs into the classroom, commit crimes, and drop out of school. They are more than twice as likely to abuse drugs and alcohol, commit suicide, and become teenage parents.

These startling statistics tear at our social fabric, which is why I have worked so hard in the Senate to pass legislation that encourages responsible fatherhood, to ensure that more children know what it is like to grow up with a loving father in their lives. America's mothers are heroic, but men have a contribution to make, too. No law can require men to be the fathers their children deserve, but we should enable and encourage every father to try. My father's presence at my Little League games, and his constant efforts to be there for me, meant more to me than any milestone he ever achieved in public office.

This is part of the genius of America—every father and every family has the ability to make the world a better place for our children. Here men are not only judged by their achievements at work or the choices they have made in life; instead, true greatness is judged in our children's eyes.

Yogi Berra

Perhaps one of the most popular players in baseball history, Yogi Berra won fourteen league pennants and ten World Series championships. A fifteen-time all-star and a three-time most valuable player, he was elected to the Baseball Hall of Fame in 1972.

What did I learn from my pop? I learned you better be on time. And I learned if you say you're going to do something, you better do it. Pop came from the Old Country, northern Italy. He settled in this country around 1911 and worked in the brickyards in St. Louis, where I grew up. We lived on the Hill, the Italian section, and he worked hard to support our family.

No one could've loved his family more—my mother, me, my three older brothers and younger sister. But he was old-fashioned in a strict kind of way. And he wanted all of us to work. He didn't understand American sports—to him, they were a waste of time. My brothers were real good ballplayers, but he would have none of it. So they had to quit to go to work. Not me, although Pop hated my playing ball. He always got sore if I came home dirty, and would smack me for sure if my pants were torn. I'd do anything not to get him mad if I could help it. Like when the quitting-time factory whistle blew at 4:30. I'd stop everything, even if I was batting in our pickup game, and race home. My job was to fill up Pop's tureen of beer at Fassi's, the saloon at the end of our block. If that can wasn't standing on the kitchen table full of cold beer when Pop came home, I was in trouble. So I learned never to be late. Maybe it's why I've always been early my whole life—too much bad comes from being late.

I guess Pop also taught me something else: Honor your word. Like if I went out at night after supper, he'd want to know what time I was coming home. If I said ten, he said then it better be ten. I guess what I mostly learned from my father is respect and honor. That, and it was never a good thing to get him mad.

Clint Black

Growing up as the youngest of four brothers in Katy, Texas, Clint Black has been involved in music his entire life. He has written and performed his own material since his Nashville debut in 1989, garnering numerous honors and popular acclaim along the way.

My dad has given me a lot of advice in his lifetime, but the one piece that sticks out and could probably be used by a lot of people these days is on driving. "Driving is a full-time job," he said. It doesn't sound like much, but considering how dangerous driving is and how much of it we all do—in many cases with a phone in our ear while steering with one hand—it turns out to be a very useful bit of advice. Dad was telling me about a time when he was driving to a golf course and noticed some questionable activity by the driver ahead of him on the highway. He kept an eye on the car, and indeed the driver came into my dad's lane and nearly hit him. If Dad hadn't been paying close attention he would have fallen victim to one of the thousands of car crashes that happen every year. When he finished the story, he said, "See? And you thought I didn't lead an exciting life." I said, "You don't lead an exciting life, but every now and then someone else's exciting life intersects with yours." He laughed, of course. It's one of our jokes that his life is lacking in that area. But the truth remains, driving can be a lot more exciting than it should be, and "Driving *is* a full-time job."

Bonnie Blair

One of the most decorated athletes in the history of the Olympics, Bonnie Blair won five individual gold medals in four Olympic Games in her unparalleled speed-skating career. In 1992, she received the Sullivan Award and the Sports Illustrated *Sportsperson of the Year as the nation's outstanding athlete.*

My dad was a man of very few words; in fact, we would often drive back and forth to the Chicago area (about two and a half to three hours) and he would hardly say two words. However, you knew that when he said something he meant it.

I remember a time after middle school when I went to my dad's office to get a ride home from school (he didn't work far from my school), and he introduced me to a new coworker named Patrick O'Connell. My dad said out of the blue, "This is my daughter Bonnie, and she is going to be in the Olympics and win an Olympic medal." At that point in my skating career, I only skated what we call pack style, or what is known today as short track, so I didn't even race the type of speed skating that was in the Olympics. So my first thought was that my dad was nuts! Then I just thought my dad was trying to impress this guy, it was so out of character for him to say something like that. I was embarrassed, but let it go in one ear and out the other. However, I never forgot it, and who would have thought all those years later I would have accomplished what I did in the sport of speed skating. He put a thought into a little kid's head, and she was able to turn it into reality. It meant a great deal for me to have him witness my first win in Calgary in 1988, to see his face and the smile he had. I don't think I ever remember seeing my dad as happy as I did that day. He died of lung cancer the following year. In my next Olympics, in Albertville, I dedicated my first win to my dad's memory, as it was his dream for me to become an Olympic medalist before it was mine. At my last games, in Lillehammer, Norway, I got a fax from Mr. O'Connell that said, "Boy, was your dad right all those years ago."

My dad was always there for all of us kids in whatever we did—baseball, swimming, softball, skating, you name it. He also volunteered his time to help out with whatever we did, whether it be sitting on the board of something, or helping with practices, or his greatest pleasure, being a timer. He was always kidded about having a fast watch when his kids raced.

I didn't want to go out for the swim team the summer following sixth grade. I can remember dreading for months having to tell my dad I didn't want to do it. I thought he would be bummed because he wouldn't be a timer and be involved himself. When the day came when he asked me if I was going out for the team, I said, "I don't think I want to," and he said, "Okay." That was it, no questions why or trying to talk me into it or anything. You see, I didn't want to swim because I didn't like getting into a cold pool (this was before heated pools), but yet I will skate outdoors in cold weather . . . I know it doesn't make sense. I obviously knew that swimming wasn't my love—I guess I like my water frozen. When people find out I got involved in skating at such a young age, I think they think I was forced into it, but that is a perfect example of my dad giving me all the opportunities but never forcing me into anything. I went into it with my heart and it was my choice; he was just there with his watch and his quiet way of being there no matter what.

I can also remember during my short-track years, when he would be a timer on the side of the rink, he would say, "Now go." That was his way of saying it was time for me to make my move and make a pass. He wouldn't yell—my dad never yelled—it was just him using his normal voice, but it was a voice I heard no matter what. That also seems kind of strange, him being as quiet as he was.

I hope I can pass on what I gained from my dad to my children, Grant and Blair Cruikshank. I only wish they knew their grandpa, but it will be up to me to share the stories with them. I truly miss those few words he would say in his quiet way.

Ken Blanchard

The author of seventeen books on management, Ken Blanchard is a much-sought-after motivational speaker and business consultant. His book The One Minute Manager, *cowritten by Spencer Johnson in 1981, continues to hit bestseller lists. His books have been translated into dozens of languages and have sold millions of copies worldwide.*

My father, Ted Blanchard, was a great leadership role model who had a tremendous impact on me. He was a classic example of the Greatest Generation. He grew up in Highland Falls, New York, a small town just outside the gate of West Point, the U.S. Military Academy. Dad loved West Point and all the pomp and circumstance surrounding it. But when he graduated from high school, his father, a doctor in town, said, "Son, I think you should go away to school."

Because he couldn't go to West Point, my father decided to go to the Naval Academy in Annapolis, Maryland.

When he graduated in 1924, my father found that in a world that believed it had just fought "the war to end all wars," there was little need for naval officers. So, after his senior cruise, he entered Harvard Business School, where he majored in finance, and ended up working in New York City. In the early 1940s, he was being groomed for a vice presidency with National

City Bank when one day he came home and said to my mom, "Honey, I quit today."

"You did what?" my mother replied.

"I quit," Dad said. "I told you when we got married that if the country ever got in trouble, I felt I owed it something. Hitler is already a threat to world peace, and it's only a matter of time until Japan gets into the fray, so I reenlisted."

This was quite a shock for my mom. I was one year old, and my sister, Sandy, was three, and just when Dad was starting to make good money, he opted for a lieutenant's salary in the Navy. Mom went along with it as graciously as she could.

In spite of my father's zest for action, his first assignment was the Brooklyn Navy Yard. Pearl Harbor came along, and still no change. When it looked as if he'd be stuck in dry dock for the duration of the war, he called one of his former classmates—who happened to be head of the Naval Bureau of Personnel in Washington, D.C.—and asked him what he had for an old-timer with no experience. A week later, his friend called him back.

"Ted, all I have for a guy with your background is a suicide group going into the Marshall Islands," he said.

My dad jumped at it—without telling my mom about the suicide part, of course. They gave him command of twelve LCIs (landing craft, infantry). With only small guns to protect themselves, Dad's unit was responsible for protecting the marines and frogmen (the SEALs of today) heading toward beaches defended by the Japanese. My dad's friend had been right in calling this a suicide mission; it was one of the most dangerous actions of the campaign. Seventy percent of Dad's men were killed or wounded. His ships were so close to the beaches that Dad's picture was in *Time* magazine one week: It showed him conducting funeral services for some of his men who'd been hit by shells that fell short after they were fired from our big ships.

I was five years old when the war ended. My mother dressed me up in a sailor suit and we went down to the train station to greet Dad, whom I essentially hadn't seen for three years.

After the war, Dad decided to continue in the Navy as a career officer. In war and in peacetime, my father was a special kind of military leader with an enlightened philosophy. He was not the typical "my way or the highway" commanding officer. He was deeply committed to both his missions and his people.

I got a good sense of this after I was elected president of my seventh-grade class. That day I came running home from school all pumped up. My father said: "Congratulations, son. It's great that you're the president of the seventh grade, but now that you have that leadership position, don't use it." My father continued, "Great leaders are followed because people respect them and like them, not because they have power." That was a pretty powerful lesson for a young kid beginning to be interested in leadership.

I learned another major leadership lesson from my dad in 1959 when I was an undergraduate studying government at Cornell University. That year my father decided to retire early from the Navy as a captain, even though he could have stayed on and been promoted to admiral.

I said, "Dad, why did you quit early?"

He answered, "Ken, I hate to say it, but I liked the wartime Navy better than the peacetime Navy. Not that I like to fight, but in wartime we knew what our purpose was and what we were trying to accomplish. The problem with the peacetime Navy is that nobody knows what we are supposed to be doing. As a result, too many leaders think their full-time job is making other people feel unimportant."

That made me realize that leadership is about going somewhere. If your people don't know where you're going, your leadership doesn't matter. Even Alice in Wonderland learned that when she found herself at a crossroads in the woods and asked the Cheshire cat which way she ought to go. The Cheshire cat said, "That depends on where you want to get to." She said she didn't much care. He said, "Then it doesn't matter."

If you want people to follow you, they need to know where you're going.

My father eventually did become an admiral, because Congress passed a law that said if you got the Medal of Honor or the Silver Star during World War II, the government would "bump you up" one rank upon your retirement. Since Dad got two Silver Stars, he became a retired rear admiral.

Admiral or not, my father certainly made a difference in my life and was an inspiration for what has become my life's journey—helping people and organizations lead at a higher level.

Brian Boitano

During the 1988 Olympics in Calgary, Brian Boitano won the gold medal and catapulted to international fame when he executed what is considered by many to be the best performance in the history of figure skating. He then turned professional, winning five consecutive World Professional Figure Skating Championships.

At the age of just fourteen, my dad started supporting his family by working in the local cannery. At the same age, I won my first national ice skating title and began competing internationally at the junior level.

At the age of twenty, my dad was drafted into the U.S. Army and served on the front lines in Germany during World War II as a medic, treating wounded soldiers. At the age of twenty, I was competing in my first Olympics in Sarajevo.

At the age of twenty-four, my dad came home from the war and went to work in banking. At the age of twenty-four, I was able to compete for a gold medal for my country in Calgary.

My dad taught me the importance of integrity and the value of a strong work ethic. My father's sacrifices and unconditional love made it possible for me to live out my dream, and the lessons I learned from his example have proved to be invaluable to me.

Pat Boone

Pat Boone is a vocalist whose versions of early rhythm-and-blues and rock-and-roll hits were instrumental in bringing that music to a mainstream audience. Known for his smooth style, Boone was a teen idol in the 1950s before turning to gospel music.

My dad, Archie Boone, was an architect, a builder. He and his much-respected Boone Contracting Company bid on, drew the blueprints for, and built office buildings, churches, schools, and homes all over middle Tennessee. During World War II, though I was just a little boy, I remember Mama looking after my brother and two sisters and me while Daddy was off in Smyrna and other places building barracks for our military.

Though Daddy and his company erected many wonderful buildings that stand as monuments to him today, he did something even more dramatic. He built a family, and instilled character in each of his four kids.

And it wasn't so much in what he said, though he was intelligent and wise and funny; his actions spoke loudly and unmistakably to us even more than his words. For much of my youth, he worked six days a week, it seemed, though Saturday nights were often family nights for bowling and the occasional movie. Sunday was for church—both morning and evening services—and often leisurely family visits.

But though he worked so long and hard, I don't remember ever being up before him on any weekday morning. Even if I got up at 6:00 or 6:30 a.m., I'd find Daddy at the dining room table with an open Bible, making notes and preparing for his Sunday school class, which he taught to young adults for most of his life. Get this—he only taught a forty-five-minute class, but he spent at least six hours of study and preparation for that forty-five minutes! And not only that: When I eventually sat in on his class a few times, I discovered that he used the Socratic method of teaching. He'd introduce a thought from the lesson and then ask for questions and reactions to the thought.

He listened—and though he had prepared much

36

harder than any of the students in the class, it appeared he was willing to learn from them any insights they might have on the topic at hand. This made a terrific impression on me.

My brother and sisters and I all knew that Mama and Daddy loved us deeply, more than anything in the world. But beyond that, we could *see* that they loved God most of all, and that learning and serving him better was the most important part of their lives. And that told us that it should be the most important part of our lives, as well.

Archie and Margaret Boone lived their last several years in a lovely nursing home in Nashville. Daddy was almost ninety-four and Mama almost ninety-one when they slipped away to heaven within six weeks of each other. And even in the nursing home, at that advanced age, they studied their Bible together and compared notes, and Daddy listened.

I strongly suspect he's still listening—learning and listening to his Father in heaven.

Scotty Bowman

Having amassed a record 1,244 victories and nine Stanley Cup titles during his thirty-year career, Scotty Bowman is the most successful coach in the history of the National Hockey League. In 1991, he was inducted into the Hockey

Hall of Fame in recognition of his exemplary work in building the game.

My father's name was John Bowman, but everybody knew him as Jack. He was an immigrant from Scotland who came to Canada in 1929 as a blacksmith. He later joined a company in 1934 after the horses went out of business. The most memorable lesson I learned from my father stems from the fact that he worked thirty-one years without missing a day of work. We couldn't even miss school all the way through. If we had a cold or some little ailment, he'd just send us off because it was normal that we report every day and he assumed we'd feel better as the day went on.

He was very proud that he went thirty-one years without missing a day of work for any reason. He worked until they retired him at age sixty-five, and he lived until he was ninety-two. He had a long life and he worked very hard.

That was the lesson that sticks from the many lessons he taught me. He passed that work ethic on to me and my two brothers and sister as well. I didn't go thirty-one years without missing a day, but I tried.

Bernie Brillstein

A highly successful producer, manager, and consultant who has handled such clients as Jim Henson and John Belushi, Bernie Brillstein operates the Brillstein-Grey Entertainment production team with his partner, Brad Grey. He has served as executive producer of many successful movies, including Ghostbusters *and* Happy Gilmore.

I t was 1967—I was thirty-six years old, and my company (Management III) wanted me to go to California to open up an office there.

My mother, who had been mostly bedridden for twenty years, was at Doctor's Hospital. Most of my relatives were shocked that I would go to California while my mother was ill. The guilt was really growing within me, and I didn't know what to do. One day my dad, Moe, asked me to take a walk with him. We were walking through the corridors of Doctor's Hospital when he suddenly stopped me, grabbed hold of my shoulders, and said, "If you don't want to end up like me, get out of here quick." Then he hugged me and kissed me good-bye.

My mother passed away two years later. By that time, my business had really started to take off. If it weren't for my dad, I'd probably be working in the garment center today.

From the time I was very young, my dad always told me to keep my fingernails clean. Because when

39

you meet someone new, if the first thing they see are dirty fingernails, their opinion of you won't be too hot.

I taught this to my children and everyone else I love. I've never forgotten it.

Dr. Joyce Brothers

Dr. Joyce Brothers has been a dean of American psychologists for more than three decades. A noted radio and television personality, she is a regular columnist for Good Housekeeping *magazine. Her syndicated columns appear in more than 175 newspapers and are read by millions all over the world.*

My father had two daughters, no sons. One is me, a psychologist, and the other is a judge. It is no news that boys need a father, a responsible, loving role model who can teach them to be tender as well as tough. There are endless stories, plays, and films about the bonds between fathers and sons, but relatively few about the major part fathers play in terms of daughters. For many years, the strength of the paternal influence on girls was forgotten. My dad did for his two daughters what studies have started to reveal—that is, the powerful impact that fathers have on all high achievers. Good fathers not only give daughters love and affection, they also teach them to be daring. Fathers teach daughters that they can succeed, that they have what it takes to fulfill their dreams in a world in which what they do and where they go in their future is up to them. And that if they do their homework and focus on learning, their choices are limitless.

Helen Gurley Brown

An author, a publisher, and a businesswoman, Helen Gurley Brown was editor in chief of Cosmopolitan *magazine for thirty-two years. During the 1960s she was an outspoken advocate of women's sexual freedom, claiming that women could have it all, "love, sex, and money." Due to her advocacy, the liberated single woman was often referred to as the "Cosmo Girl."*

After I was ten years old, I didn't have a father to learn anything from. One day, he was racing for the elevator in the Arkansas state capitol building in Little Rock. The elevator was just leaving when he got there—he jumped on and got crushed to death. People later told my mother that the Arkansas state legislature had appropriated money for a new elevator but the money had mysteriously gone other places. However, I did have experiences with him before that.

When I was nine years old, he helped me write an

essay on cotton. He sat down with me with a piece of paper and a pencil and we made notes, then I went away and wrote the essay in my own handwriting. Since it wasn't for publication in the *Arkansas Gazette,* the result was totally satisfactory, and I would have to say I got my writing start from my father. He was fabulous with people of every age and occupation. That surely included all the neighborhood kids, whom he would sit around with and tell stories to—he was a real crowd-pleaser. He was going to run for secretary of state of Arkansas the year he died; people in the Democratic Party liked and respected him and found an office he could run for without any previous experience. I didn't learn how to do what he did in terms of his words and listening skills with his peers, but I grew up knowing he had them; maybe a touch of crowd-pleasing is in my genes too. I learned to be good to the people around you who love you. He took my sister, Mary, and me to endless movies, and he seemed never to have missed a meal at home—he showed up! He was affectionate with my mother, though I'm not sure how cuckoo about him she was. I think she was in love with somebody else when they got married, but her family said she had to marry Ira Gurley because he would amount to something and give her a good life (he did!).

I think what I got from my father was a good life. He stayed employed after the big stock market crash in 1929 and during the Depression before he died on

June 17, 1932. He encouraged my schoolwork, was always there to help me with assignments, and was wonderful to my friends. I guess I would have to say he was a good person and, in whatever ways, that goodness got through to me and into me.

Dave Brubeck

Dave Brubeck is a celebrated composer, pianist, and bandleader whose "Take Five" is a jazz standard. The Dave Brubeck Quartet, formed in 1951, released some of the most influential modern jazz records, including Time Out, *which went platinum shortly after its release, and* Time Changes. *He still composes and performs internationally.*

My father, Pete Brubeck, was a cattleman, a number one steer and calf roper at the biggest rodeos in the West in the 1920s, and foreman of a forty-five-thousand-acre cattle ranch in northern California owned by H. C. Howard, owner of the famous racehorse Seabiscuit. The first word that comes to mind to describe my father's character is "honesty." He had tremendous energy, and one could usually hear him whistling or singing as he went about his work, which started before dawn and ended at sunset. My father was quick to anger, something I didn't particularly want to emulate, but he also had an amazing ability to explode and quickly return to his usual good-natured self, holding no grudges. This was an endearing quality. My father held no prejudices that I was aware of. His top vaquero was a Native American, and his crew consisted of typical rugged cowpokes and trail riders, some of Mexican origin, all of whom he considered friends. When I was a small child, he took me to see an elderly black man who had been a slave. He asked the man to open his shirt. He said, "Show Dave the brand on your chest." I knew about cattle and branding, so I understood and was horrified. My father said, "This should never happen again."

I never wanted to leave the ranch life when I was young, and my father and I were partners in the cattle business. Both of my older brothers had graduated from college and had become music teachers. I was my dad's last hope. It must have been very difficult for him when I told him that I, too, wanted to be a musician. His understanding answer was "If it ever becomes too difficult to make a living, Dave, remember you can always come back to our ranch, and we will always be partners." That promise held me in good stead when I was starting my career and the going was tough. My father epitomized the man I hoped to be—honest, courageous, determined, cheerful, openhearted, and open-minded.

President George Herbert Walker Bush

George Herbert Walker Bush was the forty-first president of the United States. Before becoming president, he held many public service offices, including congressman from Texas, ambassador to the United Nations, director of the CIA, and forty-third vice president of the United States under President Ronald Reagan.

A memorable lesson from my dad:
"Work hard, play by the rules, and tell the truth."

Sid Caesar

Initially a saxophonist and a composer, Sid Caesar began his career as a comedian while serving during World War II. Soon after, he appeared in film and then entered the world of television and Broadway, hosting television programs such as The Admiral Broadway Review *and* Caesar's Hour.

When I was little, my father used to say this about fighting with other kids: "Remember how you would feel. Count to ten. Then say, 'Can I talk to you for a minute?' The main thing is that you learn what I had to learn, that we all live together and have to *learn* how to live together. Take your time, let them understand you. Make friends with them—don't hit them. Try to make friends. Afterwards you can hit them! Not really. There are two *H*s: no hollering and no hitting—that only makes it worse. Try to make them understand what they just did, and how it affects you, and how it affects them. Try to reason with them. I know it's hard, but try to reason with them. And try to keep it that way."

Lloyd Carr

As head coach of the University of Michigan football team, Lloyd Carr led the Wolverines to an undefeated season in 1997, culminating with a Rose Bowl victory and a national championship.

My father taught me to appreciate the little things, like the beauty of a sunset, a sunrise, and a hard rain. He was born in eastern Tennessee, so he taught me to appreciate the beauty of the hills and valleys and the mountains of Tennessee and western North Carolina.

He was an hourly worker at McLouth Steel Corporation, which was a polluted, dirty place, but he taught me the value of hard work and to always take pride in whatever I did. He taught me to treat every other man like I would want to be treated. He taught me to say "Thank you," and he taught me to say "I'm sorry."

He was a great man.

Ben Carson, M.D.

Dr. Ben Carson became the director of pediatric neurosurgery at Johns Hopkins Hospital when he was only thirty-two. In 1987, he gained attention for separating conjoined twins who shared a section of the same brain. The recipient of numerous awards and honors, Dr. Carson sits on many governing boards, including the President's Council on Bioethics.

Most of the lessons I learned from my father I picked up during the first eight years of my life. My parents divorced when I was eight, when my mother discovered that my father had another family. I do, however, remember that he was a fun guy, and we always looked forward to him coming home from work in one of the Cadillac plants in Detroit, Michigan. He never raised his voice, and he never physically disciplined us. In fact, I remember one time very specifically when my mother gave him instructions to give us a spanking. He took us out away from her and grabbed a switch, and when we got out of her sight he threw it down and said, "You guys be good."

I must say that the lesson from that is that I never had to worry about my father being a disciplinarian. He would often let us drive—he would put us in his lap when we were little kids and let us drive the car. We always looked forward to that.

After the divorce, I perhaps learned some of the

most important lessons because I was able to witness his lifestyle. He was a man who was involved with lots of different women, with alcohol, and with drugs, and I learned what that does to a person. It enforced my resolve to stay away from those things, and I think that it made an enormous difference in my life as various temptations and situations arose. I was able to put them in perspective. Those were, perhaps, nonintentional lessons, but actually they are some of the most important things that I learned in my life. I think they have a significant amount to do with the success I have had.

Gary Carter

A former all-star catcher for the New York Mets, Gary Carter was inducted into the National Baseball Hall of Fame in 2003. Currently, he and his wife run the Gary Carter Foundation, a nonprofit organization for the well-being of children.

I lost my mother at the age of twelve. My mom was only thirty-seven. My father was a great dad who then took over both roles as father and mother.

That alone was a great influence in my life, as I had to grow up pretty quickly. I became domestic around the house, as we had our household jobs to do. My father was my coach for Little League, Pony League, and American Legion baseball. He always taught me to play the game hard and to hustle at all times.

He taught me to be courteous to my elders and to be kind to everyone; to use good manners, say "please" and "thank you," and try to put a smile on someone else's face; to live life to the fullest, but always give thanks to our good Lord for the gifts he has provided.

I love my dad and always will. He passed away just eighteen days after I found out about my election to the Baseball Hall of Fame. I miss my dad because he was a great man whom I respected totally.

Tommy Cash

Tommy Cash is a country-music singer and songwriter, and the younger brother of country legend Johnny Cash. In 1970, he released two top-ten singles, "One Song Away" and "Rise and Shine." Tommy continues to enjoy international success, performing regularly all over the world.

My daddy taught me that hard work pays off. He said to me when I was very young, "Work hard and good things will happen to you. Those who don't have the work ethic struggle all of their lives."

Judy Collins

Folksinger and songwriter Judy Collins began her life in music on the piano. She soon switched to guitar, however, and has since released some of the most important folk records of all time. She is also noted for her dedication to social activism, and she has done important work for many charitable organizations such as UNICEF.

In 1939, the year I was born, my father, Chuck, was in the second year of what was to become his thirty years of radio broadcasting. My mother, Marjorie, had met my dad on a bus in Seattle, Washington, two years earlier and fallen in love with him. He was, she said, handsome and charming, and had a voice like an angel.

He was also blind.

Daddy was born on a farm in Idaho and became extremely independent in his years growing up. He went to the University of Idaho, in Moscow, Idaho, where his fraternity brothers at Phi Gamma Delta loved to put him behind the wheel of a car and let him drive around campus, while their amazed friends stood around, shocked that a blind man would be driving a car. He studied law in college and had a successful band, and graduated summa cum laude before he went to Seattle, where he started broadcasting. His radio show, a combination of talk and music (which he played and sang, including all the songs of the great American writers Hart and Rodgers, Cole Porter, and Dorothy Fields), gave him a career, helped him and my mother raise us five children, and provided a platform for his talent, his love of literature, and his politics of humanity and inclusion. I learned about those things from my father.

I grew up hearing his voice in the morning, warming up for his radio show, singing those great songs, and being read to from every kind of author—from Herman Melville and the Brontë sisters to T. S. Eliot and Dylan Thomas. He ordered his Braille books from the Library of Congress, huge volumes of Braille writing that would, in the case of a long book like *Moby-Dick,* march up the side of the walls where they were stacked. He taught me first about music, and then about books, and music and books have filled my life, moved me and guided me, fueled my own career for nearly fifty years, and made my life joyful and productive. For all of this, I thank my father first.

I was the first of Chuck's five children. I loved to sing and to play the piano from the time I was very young, and my father made sure I had good training with fine teachers, and learned what he called "real music." He said he didn't want me to have to make my living doing pop music. "God Forbid!" was the way he put it. But he was always there for me, as was my mother, encouraging, appreciating, and supporting what I did. He was my first fan, and will always be in my heart and mind when I do what I do, which is to sing and to travel the country, making music, very much what my father did.

My father did his radio show, *Chuck Collins Calling,* for thirty years in Seattle, Los Angeles, and then Denver, and was a true pioneer of what they now call the "golden years of radio." He told me that his job, as he saw it, was to make people laugh, with his humor; to reflect, with his music; and to think, with the ideas that he talked about and the books and poetry he referred to in his radio shows. He composed his shows, writing the script in both Braille for himself and type print for his engineer.

My father taught me discipline and focus. He taught me I had to show up on time, do the work, and have the dream. He taught me I could overcome anything, as he had done. He taught me that life is about solutions to problems, and that problems will always come; I should expect them, but I could get through them. That was what he had done, and continued to do. I was watching a man who had courage, and he imparted that courage to my brothers, Michael, Denver, and David, and my sister, Holly, and me. We could do anything we wanted to, he said. He believed in miracles. He said they were invisible, but that we could trust in them. He could see these things. I realized later in my life that his vision was better than that of most sighted people I would come to know. He was unique. He was creative. He led the way, and had the true sight.

Chuck was about five feet eight inches, a handsome guy with a full head of gorgeous hair even at his death at fifty-seven. He was sometimes mistaken for James Cagney when he was broadcasting out of Hollywood, in the forties. He made his way to work on the bus, usually, and for years the driver of our bus in Denver had no idea Chuck was blind. When he found out, he offered my father the reduced rate, which Daddy refused, saying he would rather be treated like everyone else. His bravery in forging ahead in spite of what some would call his "handicap" would be a powerful message to me all my life. I watched him fight his way through life, fiercely independent, always positive, in spite of his demons, ever eager to have his children learn that the world is a wonderful place if you have the heart to give back to society, to vote (he thought if you didn't vote you lost the right to complain!), and to keep expecting the best. He always expected the best, of himself as well as of his children.

He would wake up singing, warming up his voice for the radio show. (I think of that on the many days I warm up my voice for my own shows—remembering Daddy's days, his optimism, his courage—maybe a line from a Dorothy Fields song he used to sing: "Grab your coat and get your hat, leave your worries on the doorstep.") He read extensively and voraciously, appreciated Theodore Roosevelt, and railed against Joseph McCarthy in his daily radio show. He did free shows for the Kiwanis and the Lions clubs, and shows for fund-raising efforts for the Salk polio vaccine, among other charities. He taught me the responsibilities of a performer, to put heart and soul in every moment, and never to judge an audience by its size. He used to say, "The one person there may be the queen of England; they may need your words more than you will ever know. Respect the individual, or the group, and always try to do your very best."

My father's alcoholism was the tragedy of his life, and, in part, of ours, because alcoholism is a family disease. No one understood that he had a disease, especially my father, and he fought his drinking with the same determination he employed toward every barrier in his path. And he rose above that demon, as he did all his others. He was so smart, and so creative, and such a person of dignity, of education, of energy. Today my siblings and I still think of him as a legend, a power, a force (sometimes like a gale wind!) in our lives, as well as a conundrum, complicated and unforgettable.

Throughout his life, with all his successes and his difficulties, my father had true humility. And, although he was blind, he saw more than anyone I have ever known.

My father died of an aneurysm in May 1968, as I was preparing to do a concert at Albert Hall in London. I canceled the performance and flew home to the funeral with my brother Denver. Friends and family members had all been told by my mother that no one was to wear black. Now was the time when my wonderful, baffling, extraordinary father would be able to see all the colors, all the time, and we were not to let him down.

I wrote this song in 1968, a month before the death of my father.

To my sorrow, he never heard it.

MY FATHER

My father always promised us
That we would live in France
We'd go boating on the Seine
And I would learn to dance

We lived in Ohio then
He worked in the mines
On his dreams like boats
We knew we would sail in time

All my sisters soon were gone
To Denver and Cheyenne
Marrying their grown-up dreams
The lilacs and the man

I stayed behind the youngest still
Only danced alone

The colors of my father's dreams
Faded without a sound

And I live in Paris now
My children dance and dream
Hearing the ways of a miner's life
In words they've never seen

I sail my memories of home
Like boats across the Seine
And watch the Paris sun
As it sets in my father's eyes again

My father always promised us
That we would live in France
We'd go boating on the Seine
And I would learn to dance

I sail my memories of home
Like boats across the Seine
And watch the Paris sun
As it sets in my father's eyes again

Senator Susan Collins

*Republican senator Susan Collins, from Maine, has served in
the U.S. Senate since 1997. She was born in Caribou, Maine,
and her family still owns and operates a fifth-generation*

lumber business. During her time in public office, Senator Collins has been a notable advocate for education and small business.

One of my earliest childhood memories is going with my dad to the Memorial Day parade in my hometown of Caribou, Maine. He hoisted me high above his head and from the best vantage point along the route—my dad's shoulders—I saw hats go off and hands go over hearts as Caribou paid its respects to our flag and honored our veterans for their service to our country.

I soon outgrew that privileged seat, but I have never forgotten the lesson I learned there. Like so much of what I have learned from my dad, it was a lesson taught not by words, but by the strength of his shoulders and the unique perspective they offered.

They are shoulders that have carried great responsibilities, and that were always ready to carry more. He had a family business to run—a business his family started in 1844 and that wasn't going to fail on his watch! He had a community and a state to serve—as mayor, Scout leader, Rotarian, and Maine legislator. And he had six children to raise, to provide for, to teach, to hoist up high. Somehow, he always had time for us, and for everything else. Somehow, those shoulders never tired.

From those shoulders, I learned that we all have an

obligation to serve, to make a difference. I learned that no one has the right to sit on the sidelines and let others do the heavy lifting. Although I never joined the family business, I did work with my dad when I was a commissioner in Maine state government and he was a state senator. When I was growing up, he taught me about integrity and principles. Working with him, I saw them in action.

Some Memorial Days, my dad would wear his Army jacket to the parade. As a little girl, I thought it was just an old, tattered jacket. Only as an adult did I learn the price he had paid for it—the Battle of the Bulge, a Purple Heart, and a Bronze Star. He never complained about his sacrifice, nor did he boast of his heroism. I learned that the burden of service must be borne willingly, and with modesty.

So thanks, Dad, for hoisting me up. The view from your shoulders was terrific, and the lessons I've learned there will be with me always.

Denton A. Cooley, M.D.

Founder of the Texas Heart Institute, Dr. Denton Cooley is a pioneer in the field of cardiovascular surgery, and is the recipient of numerous honors, including the Medal of Freedom. In 1968, he performed the first successful human heart transplant in the United States.

As I reflect on my father and his effect on my early life, there are several things I can recall. He was a successful and technically skilled and inventive dentist dedicated to his profession and obliged to support during the Great Depression years a family of four with two young sons. He was to my brother and me a heroic figure.

Among the lessons I learned from him was the importance of loyalty to family members. He emphasized that we should defend one another almost regardless of the situation. Family pride to him was uppermost when issues or threats occurred.

Another lesson he continually taught me was the importance of consideration for the feelings and comfort of others. He could not tolerate people who were "inconsiderate," and I learned that big word from him. For me, the word now has become "compassionate," to express kindness and concern for the welfare and happiness of others.

My father encouraged me to be ambitious and devoted to duty, and to apply myself to work and effort. He emphasized that success comes from dedication and self-appreciation. One should not be content with limited or early recognitions or trophies for athletic or scholarship attainment, but use these as encouragement and stimulation to go further in pursuit of loftier goals. He thought that being male was a gift and that one should learn to use that in one's family and social life. He did not adhere to the growing trend of feminism.

Throughout my young life, he advised me to become self-supportive and not to depend upon others. Because of the spare economic condition of the time, thrift was needed to permit the family to enjoy a reasonably modest lifestyle. Wealth to him was a state of mind and did not necessarily indicate financial achievement or a bank balance. Pursuit of education was more vital to success and personal fulfillment than any other thing.

The closing years of my father's life taught me a lesson that has strongly influenced me. He and Mother divorced when I was in college. As a result, his life—professional, social, and personal—declined. He became lonely, depressed, and dependent upon alcohol and supportive medication while his general health steadily deteriorated. He died at age sixty-four, some twenty years younger than the age his father died. I myself am eighty-five and still working. I have been determined to live a long life and become a distance runner rather than a sprinter. One's personal health is one's own responsibility and not someone else's. I believe that a person should enjoy one career, one home, one wife, and one family and make those one's priorities in life. For many individuals, that has not been achievable, but for me it has been.

Bob Costas

Bob Costas has won eight National Sportscaster of the Year Awards and seventeen Emmy Awards for outstanding sports announcing. He hosts Costas Now *as well as* Inside the NFL *for HBO. He is the prime-time host of NBC's Olympic coverage and will be the studio host when the network resumes coverage of the National Football League. He is a substitute anchor for CNN's* Larry King Live.

My father was a very smart, very funny, and very charismatic man. He was also a compulsive gambler with a temper that could blow like Vesuvius. He'd often have five or six thousand dollars' worth of action going on a weekend. This, in the 1950s and 1960s, when he made maybe thirty-five or forty grand a year. In other words, the mortgage was riding on whether Whitey Ford could get out of a bases-loaded jam or Wilt Chamberlain could (just this once, please God) make a freakin' free throw. This led to much excitement, elation, anxiety, heartache, and dark humor. Once, he put a thousand bucks on the Tigers specifically because Mickey Lolich was pitching. Lolich didn't make it out of the second inning, but the Tigers rallied from an eight-run deficit and won the game. When this news arrived, John Costas opened the desk draw, produced a large Havana cigar, took a few triumphant puffs, and then announced to his thirteen-year-old son, "Robert, just remember one thing. This Lolich is some fuckin' lefthander." Truer words have seldom been spoken.

I'd like to say that pearls of wisdom such as that have guided me through the years, but what sense would that make? Still, if I should ever cross paths with Mickey Lolich, you must admit I have an excellent conversational icebreaker at the ready. For that, and for a general appreciation of life's absurdities, I am forever grateful to my dad.

Jim Courier

A winner of a total of twenty-three singles titles and six doubles titles, Jim Courier spent fifty-eight weeks ranked as the world's number one tennis player during 1992 and 1993. During his career, he won four Grand Slam singles titles, two at the French Open and two at the Australian Open. He was inducted into the Tennis Hall of Fame in 2005.

M y father has always emphasized maximizing my ability in anything I do, whether it is academics, music, or sports. "There are a lot of talented people in the unemployment line," he told me when I was giving less than my best at anything. "Natural ability can only carry you so far," he said. "Making the most of your talent is the yardstick for success in this family."

I have taken those words to heart over the years and applied myself with vigor to my passion—tennis. I have seen a lot of amazing tennis talent fall by the wayside due to a lack of discipline over the years. That has not happened to me. My father's lessons have not permitted me to give anything less than my best, and my success has been a direct result of this philosophy. He once told me, "When you are prepared, all you have to focus on is enjoying the battle, knowing that you left nothing to chance." What my father gave me is the peace of mind to never have to look back on life with regret. It is an amazing gift.

Kathryn Crosby

An actress and a singer, Kathryn Crosby was known for much of her career as Kathryn Grant. An early success on the beauty pageant circuit, she appeared opposite many of Hollywood's biggest male stars during the 1950s. Her impressive film credits include The Phenix City Story *and* The 7th Voyage of Sinbad.

In spite of serving as a marine in World War I and participating in all sorts of hunting expeditions, my father, Emery Grandstaff, survived for one hundred years, sixty-five of which he devoted largely to sharing my fate.

I presented the first major problem when, having skipped the second and sixth grades, I was unable to grasp the intricacies of seventh-grade math. Emery had abandoned his position as a chemistry teacher, first to coach the West Columbia Roughnecks and then to accept the post of Brazoria County commissioner.

He set up an easel on our back porch and, employing a question-and-answer method similar to what is now termed "academic programming," led me through the curriculum. By the end of the year, I was my class's dominant mathematician.

Emery also taught me to clean his rifle and to sight it in. He rewarded me by taking me on a pack trip to hunt elk in Colorado, and on many other such adventures throughout the remainder of his life. He was ninety-seven when we shared our last hunt in Louisiana.

In the meantime, I had espoused a certain Bing Crosby, something of a nimrod in his own right, whom I gleefully astonished with my skill in manipulating sundry firearms.

Instead of dampening my youthful interest in acting, Emery backed me with constant encouragement, and later with unabashed pride. But for him, I would never have reached Hollywood, or achieved my heart's desire.

Norm Crosby

Norm Crosby has been a stand-up comedian for more than forty years, and often appears on celebrity roast programs. Frequently featured on television during the 1970s, he hosted the series The Comedy Shop *in 1978.*

My father sold ladies' shoes in a retail store in Boston for more than thirty years. He went to work every day in rain or snow, no matter his physical condition or his state of mind. The most important thing to him was his responsibility to his family.

I know that he could not have loved that job, but he did it: never protesting, never complaining, always with a cheerful attitude, and always giving 100 percent.

I had the extreme good fortune of being able to retire my father and move my mother and him to Brookline, a much more desirable area of Boston than Dorchester, where I grew up.

They had a beautiful apartment in a lovely neighborhood, with many friends nearby, and they were very comfortable and happy.

When my mother passed away in 1969, I brought my dad home with me from the funeral. He had a spacious bedroom, his own bathroom (for the first time in his life), and a housekeeper to make up his room, serve his meals, and tend to his needs. He was ecstatic. He spent his days lounging around the pool, playing with the kids, or coming with me to TV tapings and going out socially to parties and dinners.

I am so profoundly grateful that I could provide these things because I owed my father a great debt. Not so much for material things, but for the important lessons that he taught me. As a young man, I had studied commercial art and advertising. I was, in fact, the advertising manager for a large shoe chain with more than forty stores around the country, and I was building a very successful career.

My father obviously had a strong work ethic, yet when I told him that I was going to walk away from my position and try to become a comedian, he encouraged me. He said, "If this is what you want to do, then do it, but do it good!"

My father showed me how important it was to have patience, to make the very best of whatever gifts you have, to always try to be the best you can, and to share your good fortune with others who have not been so blessed. I think of my folks often and miss them constantly.

Chris Cuomo

The youngest son of former New York governor Mario Cuomo, Chris Cuomo is an award-winning correspondent for ABC News. After working as a political policy analyst for CNBC, MSNBC, CNN, and the Fox News Channel, Chris joined ABC in 1999 and was named coanchor of Primetime *in 2004.*

I t is at once a simple and all-encompassing ideal, and my pop has spent my entire life preaching, teaching, encouraging, and most of all showing me how to follow this directive. In sports, it meant playing hard (which he does) but fair (which he doesn't always, some say), dedication to team, and trying to be your best (and not being satisfied with anything less than that). At work, it meant doing something with my life that had aims and goals bigger than mere satisfaction for myself, and of course to always ask why: to question myself, my motivations and decisions, and certainly to question these same things in those around me.

But most of all my pop's instruction has helped (and continues to help) me develop my sense of devotion to my friends and my family: to do the right thing by them as brother, friend, and now husband and father. Pop has taught this through his good example, as well as by being honest enough to point out mistakes he has made, and telling me how to avoid doing the same.

He is my father, my friend, and my teacher. Certainly, he has always done the right thing by me.

Mario Cuomo

The longest-serving Democratic governor of New York in modern history, Mario Cuomo twice set New York records with the highest popular vote ever achieved in statewide elections. He is a partner in the New York City law firm of Willkie Farr & Gallagher.

My father came here from Italy just before the Great Depression. He wound up running a small grocery store in a poor polyglot immigrant neighborhood in Jamaica, Queens.

One night near the end of a difficult political campaign I appeared to be losing badly, and was tempted to feel sorry for myself when I glanced at a picture of Poppa on my bedroom bureau.

I couldn't help wondering what Poppa would have said if I had told him I was tired or—God forbid—that I was discouraged. Then I thought for a few minutes about how he dealt with hard circumstances. A thousand different pictures flashed through my mind—he was so used to dealing with hard circumstances. Almost everything was hard.

But one scene in particular came sharply into view.

We had just moved into Holliswood from behind the store. We had our own house for the first time; it even had some land around it, even trees—one, in particular, was a great blue spruce that must have been forty feet high.

Holliswood was hilly. Our house sat ten or fifteen feet above the road itself, and the blue spruce stood majestically like a sentinel at the corner of our property, where the street made a turn, bending around our property line.

Less than a week after we moved in there was a terrible storm. We came home from the store that night to find the great blue spruce pulled almost totally out of the ground and flung forward, its mighty nose bent in the asphalt of the street. My brother, Frankie, and I knew nothing about trees. We could climb poles all day; we were great at fire escapes; we could scale fences with barbed wire at the top— but we knew nothing about trees. When we saw our spruce, defeated, its cheek on the canvas, our hearts sank. But not Poppa's.

Maybe he was five foot six if his heels were not worn. Maybe he weighed 155 pounds if he had had a good meal. Maybe he could see a block away if his glasses were clean. But he was stronger than Frankie and I and my sister, Marie, and Momma all together.

We stood in the street looking down at the tree. The rain was falling. We waited a couple of minutes figuring things out, and then he announced, "Okay, we gonna push 'im up!" "What are you talking about,

Poppa? The roots are out of the ground!" "Shut up, we gonna push 'im up, 'e's gonna grow again."

We didn't know what to say to him. You couldn't say no to him—not just because you were his son, but because he was so sure.

So we followed him into the house and we got what rope there was and we tied the rope around the tip of the tree, and he stood up by the house, with me pulling on the rope and Frankie in the street in the rain, helping to push up the great blue spruce. In no time at all we had it standing up straight again!

With the rain still falling, Poppa dug away at the place where the roots were, making a muddy hole wider and wider as the tree sank lower and lower toward security. Then we shoveled mud over the roots and moved boulders to the base of the tree to keep it in place. Poppa drove stakes in the ground, tied rope from the trunk to the stakes, and maybe two hours later looked at the spruce, the crippled spruce made straight by the ropes, and said, "Don't worry, 'e's gonna grow again."

John Daly

After turning professional in 1987, John Daly won the PGA Championship in 1991 and the British Open in 1995. He set a record in the sport by winning the driving distance crown

eleven times. He has also been an active member in many
American charities, such as the Make-a-Wish Foundation.

My dad, John F. Daly, died in 1984, and it still hurts. However, I know he's there when I listen to a Puccini opera or when I forget to turn off a light because he echoes in my mind, "It's seven cents a kilowatt hour." Only a child of the Depression could know the kilowatt rate. But where I see my dad the most is in my friends. I hope more than anything that this journey will make you rich in friends—it was something my father taught me.

Because my sister, Cecilia, was born with Down syndrome, Dad became politically involved in issues involving care for the mentally handicapped. He was eventually named by the governor of Connecticut to be a member of a special board on mental retardation. Dad was passionate and boisterous about a number of issues. One of the board members told me, "Your dad was tough in those board meetings. He would get so angry at other board members about some of their proposals." But he said when those meetings were over, Dad was always the first person to round everyone up for dinner and drinks. And he was able to forget the arguments and enjoy everyone, including the people he so vehemently argued against. Some became good friends. Dad always believed no matter what your disagreements were with someone, it mattered little as long as you could share conversation, a good meal, and a good drink with them.

As a result, I am lucky to have a group of friends who span the political spectrum. I have friends who are considered Hollywood lefties; others have contributed to the so-called Swift Boat Veterans for Truth; some are moderates with varying views. My wife and I treasure the times we share with these friends. I love them all; they are there for us, and vice versa. And I talk politics and issues with most of them. And I won't lose them over an argument involving politics.

Jim Davis

Jim Davis is the creator of the popular Garfield *cartoon series. Appearing first in 1978,* Garfield *today appears in more than twenty-five hundred newspapers, a record for current comic strips.* Garfield and Friends, *an animated cartoon series, also enjoyed success from 1988 to 1995.*

My dad is a man of few words. He prefers to preach by example.

Having grown up on a farm in Indiana, I acquired a strong work ethic early on. Dad felt a boy should be able to do regular chores by the time he was ten. My brother, Doc, and I couldn't wait to be old enough to get to go to the barn with Dad.

We worked hard and had a lot of laughs as we learned a few of life's lessons. Dad always said, "If you do something, do it right." If he said, "Take two or three bales of hay to the open barn," he meant four. The manure from the barns was spread on the fields, and, after rotary hoeing, we weeded the corn rows with care, by hand. That's why Dad was the first in the county to get more than a hundred bushels per acre.

When Dad said, "We take care of our own," he didn't mean just our family, he meant the community. In a bad crop year, it wasn't unusual for us to share food with less fortunate neighbors. If a neighbor was injured or fell ill, Dad was always there to help take over his chores and whatever needed to be done in the fields.

Dad and Mom are now in their eighties and have since sold the farm and live on three acres nearby. Dad still grows flowers and vegetables. He's still farming . . .

As hard as I work, I'll never work as hard as Dad. As good a person as I try to be, I'll never be as good as Dad . . . and that's how it should be.

Frank Deford

A six-time U.S. Sportswriter of the Year honoree, Frank Deford appears on HBO's Real Sports with Bryant Gumbel *and on National Public Radio. His columns appear in* Sports Illustrated.

Honor. My father taught me honor—simply to be an honest man and not to lie. It was important to him that wherever I was, I be honest with the people I work with. The term "gentleman" is an old-fashioned word, but a gentleman is an honorable person. Honor guides you—it's the star you steer by. I know that is somewhat old-fashioned, but it's what he left with me and what I have steered by.

My father was Benjamin Deford, but people called him Benji. He didn't have a whole lot of money, but he made certain he sported a boutonniere when he went to work each day. It was important to my father that he "look the part."

He was an executive in a small company, but he taught us that everyone was the same. It didn't matter if it was the company president or the floor sweeper—my father treated them both alike. He was in charge of labor relations, and when he retired, the union officials, who were ostensibly his adversaries, gave him a plaque that read, "To a Gentleman." Whatever their differences, he maintained his civility and gentility.

In a world of increasing cacophony and tackiness, Benji Deford was a true gentleman.

Alan Dershowitz

One of the nation's foremost appellate lawyers, and a renowned attorney and Harvard law professor, Alan Dershowitz has defended O. J. Simpson, Patricia Hearst, and Claus von Bülow. His articles have appeared in the New York Times *and his many books include the number one* New York Times *bestseller* Chutzpah.

My father's name was Harry Dershowitz, and, although he never spent a day in college, he was wise beyond his education. He had street smarts and street ethics. He hated bullies and despised cheats. He always taught me the following: "Always fight up, never fight down." He meant that I should always fight with people who are more powerful, more influential, and stronger than I am. "It's better to lose to a better fighter than to beat a poorer one," he would say. Though he had in mind the kind of street fights that he frequently engaged in, as the physical protector of his family from neighborhood thugs and bullies, I have lived by his lesson in the very different kinds of fights that I frequently engage in. I try to take on presidents, chief justices, and other prominent people, rather than those in lesser positions of authority. I resist the temptation to go after people who are weaker or less powerful, though I sometimes fail to heed my father's advice.

I have tried to teach my children and my students

my father's lessons. Sometimes I succumb to the temptation to take the easy way, but when I resist—as I generally do—it is because I hear my father's soft but powerful voice. My father's way is not the easy way. Fighting up produces more losses than fighting down. But the gratification of winning is far greater, as is the importance of aiming at a more powerful target.

My father developed Alzheimer's at a relatively young age, and so I cannot be sure that he saw me living by his lessons, but I think he knew because he always supported me in my endeavors, even when they were controversial and unpopular.

My father suffered many bruises for fighting stronger enemies, but his wise advice has stood me well in my confrontations.

Phyllis Diller

Phyllis Diller is a comedian who has made countless appearances on film, stage, and television in her fifty-year career. She is well known for her work with Bob Hope, with whom she costarred in twenty-three television specials and three films during the 1960s. She is also a bestselling author and an accomplished pianist.

My dad was a beloved man, a talented salesman, a gentleman, and a good husband and fine father.

His insurance pitch was a tightly edited monologue with a beginning, a middle, and an end. He explained to me: When it is over, don't say another word. Let the person think.

You may have noticed—I never do encores.

Congressman John Dingell

One of only three men to serve fifty or more years in the U.S. House of Representatives, John Dingell is known as the "Dean of the House" for having served the longest tenure in the 435-member body. He won his father's congressional seat through a special election held after his father passed away while in office.

M y dad was small physically. He was about five feet six inches and weighed 110 pounds soaking wet, but he had a voice loud enough to fill the House chamber—without a microphone! Years before he became the first "Congressman Dingell," he was diagnosed with tuberculosis; the doctor who treated him told him he had just six months to live. From that moment on, he never took a clear breath again, but he still outlived the doctor (who, by the way, was also my godfather). He was a man who spent his life exceeding expectations. No matter what his height, weight, or health, no one could match his will. His inner strength transformed that little Pole with a bent nose into a man of tremendous gravitas.

Dad was not driven by fame, wealth, or power. My father believed in social justice. He was a man of enormous courage, determination, and decency who wanted to make life better for those who had the least. He taught me that leaders had a responsibility to protect those who struggled to protect themselves. That was one of the principles that guided him as one of the authors of Social Security. He led the fight for legislation that would have created universal health care—an idea that, as his successor, I have spent fifty years pushing for. I hope I also got a little bit of my father's will, power, courage, and determination.

When I was a boy, we used to fish and hunt together, and those times are among my most cherished memories. Dad and I talked about the need to protect and conserve fish, wildlife, the waters, and open spaces. I followed his great work on the Dingell-Johnson Act with legislation to protect endangered species, our air and water, and migratory birds. Protecting our wild spaces in Michigan, like the Detroit River and Lake Erie wetlands, was precious to him.

Things I learned at his knee have made it possible for me to work effectively for social justice and Medicare, as well as something that I know would please him: the Detroit River International Wildlife Refuge. This currently provides protection to twenty-five hundred acres of land along the Michigan shoreline—and I believe that number will grow. The waters there will be a place where generations of Michigan fathers can teach their boys how to hunt, fish, and cherish the wild places—just the way my father did with me. It would be meaningful to Dad, as it is to me, that other boys have the same opportunity to share the joy with their fathers that I shared with mine. Knowing that this vision will survive both of us means the world to me.

Bob Doerr

Bob Doerr is a former all-star second baseman for the Boston Red Sox. After entering the majors in 1937, he played in the same lineup as baseball greats Jimmie Foxx and Ted Williams. A consistent slugger and a talented fielder, he was inducted into the National Baseball Hall of Fame in 1986.

My dad had a great bearing on my life. When I was a young boy, he saw that I liked playing baseball. He saw that I got to practices, and he was at all the games I played in. This was during the Depression days, and I always had a glove and baseball shoes. He would also help other kids with gloves and shoes, such as Mickey Owen.

My dad had been a prizefighter in his younger

years. He said not to smoke, as it wasn't good for me. I never smoked at any time.

There was never a time when I left home to go play ball each year with the Boston Red Sox that I didn't kiss my dad good-bye. There was always a lot of love in my family.

My dad kept a scrapbook for me for almost every game I played in, including American Legion, high school, and all my professional games, including all of the box scores and write-ups that I enjoy looking at now. I guess you would call it a labor of love.

Ted Williams used to come to our home when we played at San Diego in 1936. He would say so many times, "Bobby, how lucky you are to have such a wonderful dad."

I thank God that I had so much love and help from my dad.

Micky Dolenz

Micky Dolenz is an accomplished actor, musician, and television and theater director. He is best known for being one of the Monkees, starring in the sitcom beginning in 1965 and providing lead vocal and drums on such hits as "Last Train to Clarksville" and "I'm a Believer."

When I was asked to contribute to this book, I was at a bit of a loss. My father died when I was only seventeen, and my memories of him have faded accordingly. It was only after some considered thought that I was able to distill from those few short years the contribution he had made to my character and core beliefs.

A very brief biography is in order.

George Dolenz was born in northern Italy at the turn of the last century and grew up during World War I. He saw his mother killed by a hand grenade, lived off turnips for six months, then fled to the United States, where he lived as an illegal immigrant until an amnesty in the thirties.

He worked his way across the States as a waiter, ending up in Hollywood as the maître d' of the world-famous Trocadero nightclub. It was there that Howard Hughes "discovered" him and signed him to a movie contract. He ended up starring in his own TV series, *The Count of Monte Cristo,* and owning a five-star restaurant on Sunset Strip.

The things I learned from my father:

The importance of having a job, making your own way, and not living off your friends, family, or the state. *[Very helpful for self-esteem.]*

That when preparation meets opportunity, wonderful things can happen. *[Very helpful in business.]*

How to cultivate the land, plant seeds, and grow crops. *[Very helpful in learning patience.]*

How to ride a horse and care for animals. *(Very helpful in my relationship with nature.)*

How to fix things when they are broken instead of throwing them away. *(Very helpful in relationships with people.)*

How to chop wood, carry water, tend a fire, hunt and fish, and survive off the land. *(Very helpful in emergencies and on camping trips.)*

How to hammer a nail by letting the tool do the work. *(Very helpful in my golf game.)*

An appreciation of music and the importance of practice. *(Also very helpful in my golf game.)*

That there are two words in show business—"show" and "business." And that you had better be pretty good at both.

Rita Dove

Rita Dove served as the U.S. poet laureate and as a consultant to the Library of Congress from 1993 to 1995. Her collection of poems Thomas and Beulah, *published in 1986 by Carnegie Mellon University Press, won her the Pulitzer Prize for poetry in 1987. She is currently the Commonwealth Professor of English at the University of Virginia.*

Flash Cards

In math I was the whiz kid, keeper
of oranges and apples. *What you don't understand,
master,* my father said; the faster
I answered, the faster they came.

I could see one bud on the teacher's geranium,
one clear bee sputtering at the wet pane.
The tulip tree always dragged after heavy rain
so I tucked my head as my boots slapped home.

My father put up his feet after work
and relaxed with a highball and *The Life of Lincoln.*
After supper we drilled and I climbed the dark

before sleep, before a thin voice hissed
numbers as I spun on a wheel. I had to guess.
Ten, I kept saying, *I'm only ten.*

Hugh Downs

*A celebrated American television host, Hugh Downs is best
known for being a coanchor of the Emmy Award–winning
ABC prime-time news show 20/20 until his retirement in
1999. He has also worked as the host of NBC's* Today Show.
*In addition, he is a member of the board of governors of the
National Space Society.*

M ost of what my father taught me was by example, rather than any kind of preaching.

When I was very little, there was no doubt in my mind that he (a) owned everything, (b) was infinitely wise and capable as well as immortal, (c) could solve any problem and overcome any obstacle, and (d) for some reason was good to me.

On top of this, he paid me the compliment of never talking down to me. He gave me grown-up answers to my questions, which was not only flattering but led to a keen motivation to learn, and kindled my interest in science, philosophy, and optimizing relationships with others. He also never dodged any questions. I can't remember not knowing the so-called facts of life.

Along the way I learned the following lessons:

1. That he did not own everything.
2. That it was not necessary to be triumphant over others to have a successful life. (As a result of this, I never felt competitive toward any colleagues in my profession. I learned that extending help to them resulted in help from them, and life seems to offer more opportunity through cooperation than through aggressive rivalry.)
3. That the universe is not out to get us. It will give you no quarter, but it is not hostile, and in the end you will be taken care of.

I had the privilege of knowing him for sixty-one years, and it was with a sort of shock that I learned that he was not immortal (and maybe for the first time realized I wasn't, either).

His legacy is simply the kind of life he led, the kind of role model he was. There may have been better fathers, but not only have I never met any, I have not read about them.

Michael Dukakis

Born to Greek-immigrant parents in Massachusetts, Michael Dukakis is a politician and former Democratic presidential candidate. He was first elected governor of Massachusetts in 1974 and also served in the office from 1983 to 1990. He ran against George H. W. Bush in the 1988 presidential election.

My dad came to this country from a predominantly Greek town in western Turkey in 1912. He was fifteen at the time, and he didn't speak a word of English. Fortunately, he had two older brothers in Manchester, New Hampshire, to ease the way a bit for him. They settled in Lowell, Massachusetts, a big mill city on the banks of the Merrimack River, and they brought the rest of the family to America, including my dad's younger brother, who subsequently became Olympia's father, in 1916.

How my father made the journey from immigrant boy to an M.D. at the Harvard Medical School twelve years later is a story in itself. But he never forgot the kind of poverty in which he had begun his life in his adopted country. So he was a pretty frugal guy, and he made sure his sons shared his commitment to frugality. In fact, if I heard the Greek words *"Economia, Mihali"* (Be thrifty, Michael) once, I heard them a thousand times, and they apparently stuck. Kitty says I'm the cheapest guy in America. I think she is exaggerating, but there is no question about my frugality.

But there was a larger lesson my father was trying to teach us. In essence, he helped us to understand that the richest things in life have little or nothing to do with material assets. It is family, community, and service to others that make us rich, and he was the living embodiment of that principle.

Of course, the ancient Greeks knew this long before my dad arrived in the promised land of America, for it was Pericles who famously said, "It is by honor, and not by gold, that the helpless end of life is cheered."

Marian Wright Edelman

Marian Wright Edelman founded the Children's Defense Fund in 1973. She currently serves as its president and is known for her tireless charity work worldwide. Before beginning work with the CDF, she worked for the NAACP Legal Defense Fund and many other civil causes.

The distinguished theologian Howard Thurman once described an oak tree in his childhood yard as having leaves that turned yellow and died each autumn but stayed on the branches all winter. Nothing—neither wind, storm, sleet, nor snow—dislodged those dead leaves from the apparently lifeless branches. Dr. Thurman came to understand that the business of the oak tree during the long winter was to hold on to the dead leaves before turning them loose in spring so that new buds— the growing edge—could begin to unfold. At winter's end, what wind, storm, sleet, or snow could not force off passed quietly away to become the tree's nourishment.

Daddy was like that oak tree. He and Mama hung on to their children until we could blossom on our own and always put our needs ahead of their own. When I think of him, I think of integrity, consistency, high expectations, family rituals, prayer, meals, chores, church activities, study, reading, service, and play. I think of common sense and sound choices, of sacrifice and bedrock faith, of unwavering gratitude and belief in the graciousness and presence of a Creator who gave us life, and to whom Daddy entrusted us in his will. I would have been devastated if I had ever found either of my parents not to be who I believed them to be. They never let us down.

Daddy, a gifted preacher-teacher and the pastor of our church, believed in God, in serving others, and in education. He constantly tried to be a good role model, and to expose us to other good role models. Daddy would pile us children into our old Dodge and drive us to hear and meet great black achievers whenever they came near our area. I learned to love to read because my daddy loved to read and had a study full of books he spent time with every day. Buying books to improve our minds was an indisputably higher priority for him than buying a toy or nonessential clothing. He used to ask us whether the teacher had given us any home-work. If we said no, he'd say, "Well, assign yourself some." My sister Olive reminded me recently that the only time our father would not give us a chore ("Can't you find something constructive to do?" was his most common refrain) was when we were reading. So we all read a lot!

Daddy taught us to make sound choices and to focus on the truly important things. My brother Harry tells about coming home from Morehouse College for Christmas and gently chastising Daddy for allowing the family car to deteriorate. He had a heavy social agenda planned and needed the car. He also noticed that Daddy's clothes were not up to their usual standards and that his shoes needed to be replaced. Harry called all these things to Daddy's attention. Daddy smiled and quietly replied, "My credit is good and I could trade the car in this morning. I can replace my suits and I can buy new shoes, but your tuition is due in January. I cannot do both. So I have decided to tune up the car, clean the suits, and have my shoes repaired."

Daddy died with holes in his shoes several years later. But he had three children who had graduated from college, one in college, and my brother Harry enrolled in divinity school. He also had a vision he was able to convey to me as he lay dying in an ambulance: that I, as a young black girl, could be and do anything, that race and gender are shadows, and that character, self-discipline, determination, attitude, and service are the substance of life. I was fourteen years old the night Daddy died. All of his conversation with me in his last conscious moments were of the future—about the importance of not letting anything get between me and my education.

I never once considered marrying in my early or middle twenties because I was too busy trying to make a difference, as Daddy expected. Daddy taught us by words and example that service is the rent we pay for living, the very purpose of life and not something you do in your spare time. I do today, perhaps on a larger scale, exactly what he did: serve and advocate for children and the poor. While cleaning out our house after Mama's death, I was astonished to find how many of the seeds I am still struggling mightily to harvest for children and the poor were planted during my childhood.

I was awed and humbled to find years of Daddy's saved articles and clippings on teen pregnancy, unequal educational opportunity, family values, and race relations, and sermons decrying the breakdown of family and community and the lack of attention to the neediest among us. He insisted that poverty of things is no excuse for poverty of spirit. How humbling yet comforting it was to see that my journey of discovery had both begun at and led me back home.

Among a pile of Daddy's old issues of *Christian Century* magazine was one opened to a page with a quotation by Dwight David Eisenhower underlined in red: "Every gun that is made, every warship launched, every rocket fired, signifies, in the final sense, a theft from those who hunger and are not fed, those who are cold and are not clothed. This world in arms is not spending money alone. It is spending the sweat of its laborers, the genius of its scientists, the hopes of its children." I had discovered this quotation independently in a Washington, D.C., library several years before, made it into a Children's Defense Fund poster, and used it in many speeches. How reassuring yet eerie to feel Daddy's guiding hand affirming my work for children and my struggle with misguided national priorities so many years later.

When I don't know what to do or which way to go, or feel profoundly inadequate to the task at hand, an echo of my father's frequent off-key humming of the spiritual "There Is a Balm in Gilead" wells up in my heart, reminding me that I don't have to preach like the apostle Paul or Dr. King or meet Harvard's or Yale's or Congress's or the White House's or society's decreed standards of anything to be a useful messenger or servant in the world. His example and the lessons he taught me still keep me grounded and guide my way.

Don Edwards

As a goaltender in the National Hockey League, Don Edwards had a highly successful eleven-year career that included seasons with the Buffalo Sabres, Calgary Flames, and Toronto Maple Leafs. In 1979–1980, he was awarded the Vezina Trophy for having the lowest goals against average.

My father, Arnold Edwards, taught me never to burn bridges, because at some point you'll likely have to cross them again.

When coach Scotty Bowman traded me from Buffalo to Calgary, I was extremely bitter. Buffalo was very near to my heart, so immediately I felt resentment, and you can bet there were plenty of nasty things I wanted to tell to Bowman, but I remembered what my father taught me and I resisted saying anything. Instead, once I got to Calgary and cleared my mind, I sent Bowman a letter thanking him for everything he taught me and the opportunities he'd given me. A week later, I got a letter back from Bowman, and it was comforting to my soul. So in this case, the advice my father gave me saved my relationship with Bowman. Now I still have a friend where I might otherwise have had an adversary because I didn't burn a bridge.

In 1991, I was thirty-seven years old and living back in Buffalo when my mother, Donna, and my father came to visit me. I took my father to see the Sabres play the Chicago Blackhawks. They might normally have stayed overnight, but they were eager to get back to their home in Hamilton, Ontario. My sister, who lived next door to them, had been the victim of a sexual assault and rape, and they felt they should be near her because the courts had seen fit to release the perpetrator from custody. They were fearful for her safety and for their own well-being, but they tried not to reveal their concern to us.

Six days later, their fears were realized when the stalker ambushed my sister by hiding under her stairs in the morning, and she fled into my parents' home. He blasted his way into the house with a gun and then shot my mother before stabbing my father to death. My father put up one hell of a fight, which allowed my sister to flee unharmed. I was allowed into the house afterward, and the devastation was unbelievable. My father obviously went through great pain to put himself in the forefront and protect the family. My parents made the greatest sacrifice of all—they gave their lives.

Karl Engemann

Former vice president of Artists and Repertoire at Capitol Records, personal manager for Marie Osmond for the past thirty years, and father-in-law of CNN's Larry King, Karl Engemann is also the proud father of five and grandfather of nine.

D ad came to the United States from Germany in 1906 when he was eight years old. He and his three older siblings traveled in steerage class on a steamer by themselves, as their widowed mother had come to this country four years earlier to earn enough money to be able to send for them. The captain of the ship knew of their circumstance and kept an eye out for their well-being, even giving the oldest brother (who was twelve) a job in the bakery so he could bring his brothers and sister bread and cakes.

One of my fondest memories of my father is from when I was about three years old. We were standing in front of the neighborhood corner grocery store on Fleming Street in Detroit. He was holding my hand as I stood gazing at a little boy mannequin dressed in a pinstriped baseball uniform in the front window of the store. There I was, hoping my father would buy it for me—and my father was wishing he could afford it, but it was 1933 and the middle of the Depression.

I never got that uniform, but as I grew older my father gave me so much more. He spent time teaching me how to catch and throw a baseball and how to handle a bat. There was only one bat in the neighborhood, and it had been splintered and taped and retaped many times over. The same with the baseball—only one, and if it was hit where we couldn't find it, that was the end of the ball game.

My father also taught us kids how to play "run down" or "hot box" by using some old, worn out socks rolled up and taped like a baseball so we could run the bases and tag each other out. We'd do anything to keep playing on that old homemade baseball "field of little boy dreams," where we all felt we could grow up to play for the Tigers some day.

He really couldn't afford it, but a couple of times he took me to Briggs Stadium to watch the Tigers play and see my baseball heroes of the day such as Hank Greenberg, Rudy York, Schoolboy Rowe, Birdie Tebbetts, Pinky Higgins, and Tommy Bridges.

My dad loved baseball and would play in pickup games on weekends and holidays every time he could. He was a good hitter and a terrific pitcher with plenty of "stuff," and played catcher when he wasn't pitching. I remember when he'd catch a game, he'd drive more than one batter nuts when every now and then, just as the pitch was arriving at the plate, he'd stretch his arms way out front to snatch the ball right out of the air before the batter had a chance to swing! I can hear the screams ringing in my ears even now—"You can't do that!" I remember that once when he was in his sixties he pitched in a pickup game with players much younger, some in their twenties. He threw hard that day, mostly curveballs because he'd lost the zip on his "heater" and thoroughly exhausted himself. Late that night, my brother got a call from our mother exclaiming, "Your father's fainted!" Thankfully, he recovered after having given his all.

Dad was a strong swimmer and a terrific tennis player, driving opponents crazy with his slice serves and wily ways on the court. He even had some modest figure skating moves. He was a man for all seasons. He played what was then called "trap" drums and percussion in dance bands in the 1930s and '40s. He also played violin and a little guitar. I'd go with him as he played dance jobs to watch him work, thinking that someday I'd play in a dance band. I realized that wish after I learned to play saxophone and had my own dance band while going to high school. My dad would come with us and play violin for nothing, just so he could have that experience of playing with and being near his son.

My father was a spiritual man. At the dinner table, sitting on the front porch, or traveling in a car, he'd draw us into discussions about what really makes us happy and successful in life. He did much more than "talk the talk"—he "walked the walk," serving in numerous positions of responsibility in our church and giving service to others. Dad was also a magical man as a storyteller to his kids, grandkids, and even neighborhood kids. He'd spin his own made-up stories of the old West, placing each child listening smack dab in the middle of the story. He'd let each one pick his or her own horse's color and name—and everyone became a hero!

One of the great legacies he left us, as well as countless friends and neighbors, was never failing to say "I love you" each day to every member of his family. His example even now touches many others as I'm told by them time and again how watching him with *his* family motivated them to be more open and tender about expressing love for *their* families.

My dad was a top Electrolux vacuum cleaner salesman when they first came on the market and he was making pretty good money in the late 1930s, but then World War II broke out and vacuum cleaners were considered a nonessential item. The manufacturing of the sensational new Electrolux machines came to a screeching halt. Dad then became an insurance sales-man, and this new direction brought some good times and some tough times financially—but we were never bothered by not having a lot of material things. We had so much love in our family that all the neighborhood kids always wanted to hang out at our small frame home. They said it made them feel good to be there.

When I was a little boy, I'd always worry about my father dying—getting in an accident or some other un-foreseen tragedy. He quite often worked late into the evening and sometimes wouldn't come home until nine or ten at night. When the hour got late and we started to worry, we'd sit at a window and watch, hop-ing that each car coming down Joy Road and crossing Middlebelt Road would then turn right on Fremont Street and pull into the driveway at 8875.

Sometimes he got home in the afternoon, and when he did, if my younger brothers and sister and other kids were playing stickball with a broom handle and an old tennis ball out on the gravel road in front of our house, all the neighborhood kids would see him and start shouting, "I saw him first!" Then they'd run to meet his car and jump on the running board, where he would let them ride as he drove ever so slowly.

Dad was told he had stomach cancer when he was seventy-eight years old (he lived eleven years after being diagnosed). He seemed to stay relatively strong for years, but I later learned he suffered without letting us know. Eventually, the strong dad I knew grew weaker and began experiencing heavy pain.

When I was a young boy worrying about my father dying, I would never have imagined that I would some day wish to see him go. But as his pain intensified, none of his family could bear to see him suffer. We *prayed* he'd be taken home beyond the veil to meet his Heavenly Father and greet his parents and brothers and sisters who had gone on ahead of him. Our mother survived him by another fourteen years. They both died at the age of eighty-nine.

Dad's funeral was a sweet, tender remembrance of a man full of love for his family, his neighbors, and everyone his life touched—and we were all grateful and gladdened to see him at peace. His influence and love still continue to permeate our lives. I feel him with me constantly.

We love you, Dad.

Carl Erskine

Carl Erskine is a former star pitcher for the Brooklyn and Los Angeles Dodgers. Appearing in five World Series, he helped lead the Dodgers to victory in 1955. After retiring from Major League Baseball, he moved back to his native Indiana to pursue business and coaching.

My dad was born in 1884 and, consequently, he knew life in the raw. Maybe that's why he appreciated what he had and could make something out of someone else's throwaways. For instance, his visits to the local junkyard always produced a repaired and repainted wheelbarrow, lamp, table, or other item he would find there. He never owned a new car, but his used cars always looked and ran like new ones.

Dad was a good semipro baseball player and possessed a wonderful throwing arm. His daily summertime ritual was playing catch with me and my two older brothers. We played a game called "burn out." We would start nice and easy, with each throw getting a little harder until finally they would have me pinned back against our old barn. I kept reaching higher and higher to throw harder and harder. That's how I learned to throw straight over the top, the same delivery I used for twelve seasons with the Dodgers.

I'm often asked how I developed my overhand curve, which the old-timers called a "drop." One winter evening when I was twelve, Dad was showing me how to put rotation on a curveball. As he stood in the middle of the living room, gripping a baseball and demonstrating the correct delivery with a full arm motion, he accidentally released the ball. It bounced once and went through the open door into the dining room. We heard this huge crash as it shattered the glass door in my mother's china cabinet. "Matt Erskine, what have you done?" she screamed. With a smirk on his face, he looked down at me and said, "Son, that's the biggest break I ever got on a curveball."

Bob Eubanks

Bob Eubanks is an Emmy Award–winning television host and speaker best known for The Newlywed Game. *Before entering the world of television game shows, he worked as a music promoter, manager, and disc jockey in Los Angeles. He has recently appeared in NBC's* Most Outrageous Game Show Moments *specials.*

My father was a kind and considerate man with a somewhat hot temper, but that temper was never aimed at my mother or me. He directed his anger at what he perceived to be human injustices. He had such a soft heart that both my successes and failures would always bring tears to his eyes. He wasn't a humorous man, but had a tremendous sense of humor and constantly laughed about life—seemingly inconsequential things would tickle him for months, and he always had a twinkle in his eye.

I think the lesson I learned from my father is that because I felt safe at home, I had the confidence to go out into the world, knowing full well that if I failed, I always had a safe place to go.

Jamie Farr

Jamie Farr is an actor who played the role of the wacky yet enterprising Corporal Max Klinger in the record-setting television series M*A*S*H. *He has hosted an LPGA golf tournament in Ohio, formerly known as the Jamie Farr Toledo Classic, since 1984.*

My father, Samuel N. Farah, came to the United States from Lebanon through Ellis Island. He worked as a butcher in Sioux City, Iowa, before he moved to Toledo, Ohio, and opened a market. Sometimes I worked at his market in the afternoon.

He may have had a meager salary, but he taught me that you should never be ashamed of who you are or be envious of other people. And to always appreciate what you have.

Raoul Lionel Felder

Celebrity divorce lawyer Raoul Lionel Felder is famous for his high-profile clients and highly publicized cases. He is also the author of seven books, including Divorce: The Way

Things Are, Not the Way Things Should Be *and* Getting Away with Murder. *He regularly contributes to radio and television programs for CNN and the BBC.*

I learned from my father that the most important lessons or gifts a father can pass on to a son have nothing to do with money. In my father's case, his legacy was a consuming sense of outrage. My father's life was, to my then frequent embarrassment, lived out perpetually tilting at windmills. However, as I got on in life, I realized that most of the great progress in the world is accomplished by people who rebel against the given: people who do not, robotlike, accept the status quo, people who do not accept perceived injustice, people who do not meekly get in line as one of a complacent herd.

My father, if financial achievement is the mark of a successful life, was a failure. He failed at being a veterinarian, he failed at being a lawyer. However, coming to America as a refugee from a totalitarian European state, he believed that America was the land of the possible—that wrongs could be righted, that a single person could be an agent of change.

He lived his life running for low-level public offices—always unsuccessfully—and writing to President Roosevelt, proudly displaying, whether asked or not, a form letter of acknowledgment from the White House. Lord only knows what the postman, delivering a letter in Depression-era Williamsburg, Brooklyn, must have thought when he placed the small white envelopes, with the simple return address "The White House," engraved in blue, in our mailbox.

When my father believed that there was an injustice perpetuated against him, he would sue, sue, sue. The defendants were often large corporations. He believed that the courts were the great equalizers in society, and sometimes he would actually be successful, if not because of the legal strength of his position, but through sheer obstinance and perseverance.

I think of him, and what he might do in a situation, when I become too complacent, too satisfied, too smug, or too willing to be a spectator at a wrong, too unwilling to leave the comfort of the majority and accept criticism, and sometimes I try to do what he might have done. If I can pass this on to my children, it will be more valuable to them and me than any sum of money or treasure that I can write into a will.

Garth Fisher, M.D., F.A.C.S.

Dr. Garth Fisher is a renowned plastic surgeon whose work appears on the popular television show Extreme Makeover. *He was named one of the best cosmetic surgeons in his field in Best Doctors in America, an authoritative listing of the medical world. His expertise and excellence are sought by top celebrities and businesspeople from all over the world.*

I t was the last conversation I ever had with my father and was also the last time I would see him.

I was eleven years old on that overcast September afternoon, when an incident in the basement of our home in Ithaca, New York, changed my life forever.

My father, Donald Garth Fisher, a U.S. Air Force major who had been teaching at Cornell University, had just received his orders for a highly classified reconnaissance mission in a faraway place called Vietnam.

As he hugged me tightly late that afternoon, my father told me there was a chance he might not be able to return to my mother, my sister, and me. "You need to be the 'man' of the family while I'm away." He told me that I would need to be strong and stay focused on caring for our family if that happened.

In that short and critically powerful message, my father summed up the entire legacy he would leave to me. He was right about everything he said. He would never return, and my life would never be the same again.

My mother, my sister, and I moved to live with my maternal grandparents in Laurel, Mississippi, after my dad left. We all crowded into one bedroom, which became my "home" for eight long years. What I learned about that faraway place called Vietnam came mostly from television news programs. The news from Vietnam was not good. Something had gone terribly wrong with my father's mission. He would ultimately be declared "missing in action." My family was plagued by political confusion. Multiple sightings and reports indicated that my dad was a prisoner of war. The Department of Defense disagreed. Over the next decade and a half, I desperately hunted for clues about my father's fate, and even tracked down the one surviving crew member from his destroyed aircraft, against the wishes of the Pentagon. Finally, the Department of Defense classified him as KIA, which I learned meant "killed in action." The intervals of time were painful and excruciating.

My grandfather was kind and generous to me. What he lacked in shrewdness and sophistication he made up for with integrity. My father had been a strict disciplinarian, but there was always an inner sense of compassion, a quiet, vibrant demeanor and a deep sensitivity toward his family. It was this blend of what he represented and what I can remember that I ultimately began to appreciate. I missed his guidance desperately, and wanted to do the things he'd spoken of in his final conversation with me, which I thought about often. As I grew up, I learned that honor and integrity were principles that guided my dad. He wasn't physically with me, but his spirit loomed large in my desire to conduct my life so that he would be proud of me. Financial assistance from the government was meager, and I took on many jobs to help support my family. Even as a young teenager, I tried to live by the mantra of my father's message, which would guide me for the rest of my life.

Newspaper delivery routes, washing dishes at a local restaurant, summer construction jobs, and even roofing were a few of my many jobs during junior college. I never ventured far from home during this time, as I thought my father would want me to be close to the family. It was while I attended a local junior college that I took a part-time night job as a janitor at the city hospital. There, on a chance occurrence, I accepted an invitation to observe a gallbladder operation.

That single circumstance was the event that shaped my goals and aspirations. I knew my future was to be in medicine, and I wanted not only to be a surgeon, but the best possible surgeon I could be. My father would have expected no less of me.

I was blessed during this journey to have been influenced by several surrogate fathers. Each in his own way contributed to the principles I developed. I was fortunate, as well, to have been trained by some of the finest surgeons, who imparted not only precise and masterful surgical techniques but also the art of treating patients with respect and compassion.

Often I reflected how, despite my apparent disadvantages, I journeyed from the small town of Laurel, Mississippi, to the competitive marketplace of a successful

Beverly Hills plastic surgery practice. Being selected as the initial surgeon to be featured on ABC's *Extreme Makeover* show was an incredible honor for me.

And now I've come full circle. I am scarcely older now than the age my dad was when he left us on that cool day in September. I have a wonderfully supportive family and two precious children who form the center of my universe. As I watch my two girls grow and develop, I think every day about what their lives would be like if I was suddenly taken away from them. As a physician, I recognize the value of human life, and on another, far more personal level I am cognizant that in a very special and unique sense, every day with my family is a blessing and achievement of its own.

In that wonderment, I can't help but pause and know that my father is with me today, perhaps not in the operating room, but in a larger sense guiding and directing my family life. I know that if he had never left that fateful day, he would be here, fully participating in the life of my family as a proud parent, as surely I would have wanted him to do. His last message to me, almost forty years ago, still rings true to this day. In many ways, it is a message of hope that all parents might provide to their children.

Renée Fleming

American soprano and opera star Renée Fleming grew up in Rochester, New York, in a very musical family. In 1988, she made her debut as the Countess in The Marriage of Figaro *at the Houston Grand Opera. She has gone on to countless other stellar performances at such venues as the New York City Opera and the Royal Opera House, Covent Garden.*

In my favorite photograph of my father, he is conducting a choir on the steps of City Hall in Ridgway, Pennsylvania, his arms raised commandingly in the air. His gesture makes one think of Toscanini, but his rakish good looks and the black lock of hair tumbling across his forehead recall the young Elvis Presley. Although the audience keeps a respectful distance, I am standing beside him, a tiny five-year-old, dressed to the nines in a crisp new dress with black patent leather shoes, white lace socks, and a head full of shiny ringlets. My legs are crossed awkwardly, probably in embarrassment over my boldness at having stood away from the crowd.

Looking at that image decades later, I realize that it almost perfectly illustrates what my father helped me to accomplish in life. So great was my love and admiration for this man that I would struggle mightily against my own nature in hopes of being able to please him.

My problem was that I was earnest and meek to a fault. Nothing pleased me more than spending hours alone, reading, sewing, or writing music. When I did socialize, I found that I would be devastated by something as harmless as a scowl from one of my classmates, and I would spend days analyzing the potential meaning of it, when it was most likely something he ate that was the cause. If it wasn't for my dad's pushing me encouragingly from the sidelines, I honestly don't know if I could have found the strength—the desire and the dreams were already there—to thrive in a world as exotic and colorful as opera.

I knew I could trust him in his campaign to help me become more self-confident, because as far as I was concerned, my father was perfect, and I idolized him completely. He taught high school vocal music, challenged his amateur church choirs with difficult pieces, played the piano by ear, and taught me about Bach and Brahms while somehow simultaneously fixing our cars, putting an addition onto our house, and then— why not?—even building a house. During the summer, he would take us on cross-country trips or boating on the Finger Lakes on the wooden motorboat he meticulously maintained. In my earliest memories, he hunted and fished to fill up our freezer with venison and trout. It never once occurred to me that in those days, hunting was one way to put meat on the table with a schoolteacher's salary. I believed we were wealthy, and in retrospect, we were: Ours was a family rich in love.

Looking back, a lot of my father's heroic abilities must have been born of necessity, but to him, we were just better off being self-reliant. He provided the tools for shaping my own character, rather than a cute dress. The cute dress would never increase in value, but the dividends of character were limitless. It was always clear that my father's greatest joy was spending time with us, something he did with infinite patience and the firm conviction that his children's dreams were meant to be fulfilled. When he did choose to indulge me, it was usually with animals, a gift that taught me about responsibility and gave me something that I could love and that would love me back—above all, my English setter, Bessie.

Like many young girls, though, I was obsessed with horses, so one Christmas morning Windy arrived on our front lawn. We kept him for weeks in the garage of our split-level home in a suburban tract-housing complex before the local zoning board was alerted. At my first major horse show, my dad instructed me on competitiveness, a quality girls then seldom developed, as so few of us played team sports. I had run to the Porta Potti to throw up my breakfast from nerves after having choked in the first class (gleaming new cowboy hat and bright green chaps notwithstanding). My father was not sympathetic to my fears. He told me to straighten up my cowboy hat and get out there. "If we're going to make the effort to do this, you'd better get in the ring and start trying." There was no quitting before you had even started. In fact, there was very little quitting at all.

I sometimes can't help but think that the difference between how children grew up in my generation and how I am raising my daughters speaks to one of the twentieth century's greatest social transitions. Today, as parents, we spend countless hours in conferences with teachers agonizing over a child's every unhappiness or weakness, wondering whether he or she should be tested for learning disabilities, as well as rejoicing in every success, no matter how small. Developmental psychology, at best, has enabled us to arm our children with a road map to life and with the tools for actually finding success, health, and happiness, rather than stumbling on it by accident.

When I was young, we usually learned by the example our parents set, which only occasionally involved firsthand information about the process of becoming an adult—information that was typically delivered in pearls of wisdom that we were expected to string together to form the rest of the story of who we were and what we would become. One such pearl from my father concerned intelligence. An overly sensitive, somewhat morose adolescent, I complained to him one day that a classmate had deliberately made me feel stupid, surely to shore himself up. Dad simply said that real intelligence lay in the ability to solve problems—life's genuine problems—and not in the facile knowledge that can answer some question of trivia. This advice happened to coincide neatly with my own set of natural gifts, so I stored his lesson away as guidance I cherish to this day.

My father wasn't the distant rock that so many of my friends' fathers were, but a teacher and a friend, a friend who could listen to my woes for hours, and even feel comfortable enough to express his own. In my early twenties, during a painful conversation we had about a misunderstanding regarding family loyalty, I threw down my tennis racket and complained in the shakiest of voices, "But, Dad, all I've ever wanted was to be just like you!" There is still a wallflower in my soul, but she is encased in the body of an opera singer now, decked out in feathers and diamonds. She is someone who can show up in any country, eat with any diplomat, and sing in several languages.

More recently, there was an incident in which I was practically booed off the stage at La Scala in Milan (the sort of hostile reaction from a crowd baseball heroes shrug off every day, but one for which opera singers are hardly conditioned). What helped me muster up the courage to once again get back on that particular horse, to return six months later and sing again, were my father's lessons. He chuckled, "Of course you did; you're a Fleming."

Howard Gardner

A professor of education at Harvard University, Howard Gardner developed the theory of multiple intelligences, which challenges the established criteria surrounding human development. From 1972 to 2000 he acted as codirector of Project Zero, a leading research group on psychology at Harvard's Graduate School of Education.

At first blush, my father, Ralph Gardner (who was born in Nuremberg, Germany, in 1908 and died in Brookline, Massachusetts, in 1999), and I were very different. Dad was of average height, spoke English with a heavy German accent, never went to college, spent his working life as a salesman, and was cautious, shy, and taciturn. Dad had no relation to the arts—he used to quip, "Music is the noise that bothers me the least," and I don't think that he ever went voluntarily to a museum, though he used to take me to wrestling matches and, once or twice, to vaudeville when I was young. For my part, I am pretty tall, a native fluent speaker and writer of English ("No unpublished thoughts," someone once chided me), have spent forty-five years at Harvard, love music, and devote my spare time to the arts.

My father's life was also marked by tragedy. Hitler took over Germany when Dad was not yet twenty-five. He was lucky to escape with his life; indeed, my parents arrived penniless in New York City on Kristallnacht, when less fortunate relatives were murdered in Nuremberg. Five years later, my parents lost their only child at the time, my brother, Eric, in a freak sleigh-riding accident. They later told me they felt that they had lost everything. I've been fortunate to have been spared the worst tragedies of life.

Indeed, I consider myself incredibly lucky. I managed to choose wonderful parents: Hilde Weilheimer, still very active at ninety-four, and Ralph, who died at ninety-one. Psychoanalyst Erik Erikson, my teacher, once observed, in an almost offhand matter, that successful individuals do what their mothers wanted them to do, in the ways that their fathers would have done it. From my mother, I absorbed a love of the arts, gained a sense of comfort with other individuals, and found my place in an extended family that was more intellectually oriented.

But with every passing year, I appreciate more the indispensable contributions that my dad made to my own development and to "the way that I do things." Dad was a tireless worker who always prepared thoroughly and carefully for the next challenge. In his quiet way, he cared enormously for others—whether it was taking care of family members who were victims of the Nazi regime, or of his own employees, as his book business in Scranton, Pennsylvania, prospered. He was deeply reflective about personal and professional decisions, taking long solitary strolls each day; yet at the same time, he knew how to listen carefully to others and to learn from them. After his retirement (successfully, at age fifty-eight), he used to breakfast with his cronies at Shooky's restaurant, in downtown Scranton. Because of his wide knowledge of business, finance, and politics, his soft sense of humor, and his excellent judgment in so many spheres, they called him "the Baron."

I leave for last what is by far the most important contribution that my father—and my mother—made to my sister, Marion, and me. They were the most honest people I have ever met, as well as the most trustworthy and the most loyal. They told the truth, they were scrupulous in their dealings with others, and they never thought to cross lines that too many others do, when they think that they can get away with it. If they said that they would be somewhere, or do something, they fulfilled their commitment with the reliability of the George Washington or Abraham Lincoln of legend. All too often, they would be disappointed with the behavior of others, but were more forgiving than I am inclined to be. But they made clear to me the difference between people who "got it" in terms of integrity and those who did not.

I hope that my father knew how much I appreciated all that he gave me. As I grow older, there is no greater pleasure than seeing some of his finest traits vividly present in my own four children.

Beverly Garland

A stage, film, and television actress whose work includes Playhouse 90 *and* My Three Sons, *Beverly Garland has appeared in forty-one feature films and almost seven hundred television shows. Her prolific and successful career earned her a star on the Hollywood Walk of Fame.*

I am an only child, so I suspect I received considerably more attention from my father than children who have brothers and sisters.

My father was the most positive person I have ever known. He also taught me love and how to be strong. He taught me many lessons, and two stand out in my memory.

One day at home, when I was about six years old, I remember vividly my father taking me aside. He said, "I want you to always be safe. Listen carefully. If you are ever afraid, this is all you need to say: 'Around myself and mine I draw the ring past not through, which not of evil but only good and love can come to me and mine.' "

He said I could draw an imaginary circle around me that was so powerful nothing evil could get inside it to hurt me. I believed him with all my heart!

As I grew up, I was never afraid. If I walked home from school and a stranger approached, I quickly recited my father's advice and any fears I might have had disappeared.

The other lesson from my father is more universal. He told me, "There is no such word as 'can't.'" I have lived my whole life firmly believing that.

I was really blessed. I had a wonderful dad.

Bill Gates

Bill Gates is the founder, chairman, and CEO of the Microsoft Corporation. He and his wife, Melinda, started the Bill & Melinda Gates Foundation, a charitable organization that has given unprecedented support to college scholarships, AIDS prevention, and vaccination efforts. He is also the author of several books on business and technology.

My dad always had a deep sense of responsibility to his work, to volunteering, and to his family. He was always willing to talk with us about what he was doing—even complex legal cases—and we could tell he really enjoyed what he did. He would also get very involved in our interests, taking the family on trips to cool places or helping me find books about the things I was interested in. He even went with me on Boy Scout hikes, which probably wasn't a natural thing for him to do, but he thought it was important.

Dad grew up in a family that didn't have much in the way of resources—he fought in World War II and put himself through law school, even though his own father didn't graduate from high school. He didn't talk much about it, but we always got the sense that it was very important to him for us to take advantage of all the many opportunities that we had.

My dad always set a good example for us—we learned so much just by watching how he did things, and we could tell he held us to some pretty high standards in terms of working hard, being knowledgeable and prepared, understanding the people around us, keeping organized, and taking what we do seriously. When we didn't meet those standards, his criticism was very direct and calm—in fact, he was calm about pretty much everything. He didn't criticize us often—so when he did, that made it all the more powerful.

Uri Geller

Uri Geller is a celebrated psychic whose unique powers have assisted both scientists and world leaders. He is also a popular novelist and television personality. He currently lives in England and contributes regularly to newspapers, magazines, and the Internet.

My parents had many other children, but I was the only one my father allowed to live. Years after he died, my mother told me he had forced her to have eight abortions. I had eight brothers and sisters, and my father ended the lives of each of them. Finally, he was moved by my mother's despair and pleading, and he permitted the ninth to be born alive. I believe this is the root of my psychic abilities: the energy of my sisters and brothers is channeled through me.

Throughout my childhood, I lived with a sense of fear. My father beat me when I did wrong, but he was a scrupulously fair man who did not lash out unless he believed I deserved it. The worst thrashing of my life was delivered after I stole a Torah scroll from a schoolmate. I'd taken it home and torn it up, because I felt ashamed of myself. My father's rage was terrifying. I thought he was going to kill me, and he could have done so with the buckle end of his belt as he laid into me—but for all his anger, he never lost control.

He did not lie, and I've always tried to measure up to that quality. He didn't allow his honesty to get in the way of his philandering: My mother knew he had other women, and he made no attempt to hide it. We would be eating at our tiny table in the flat in Tel Aviv, and I'd hear a whistle from the street, and my father would jump up as soon as his plate was empty. I'd run to the window and watch him saunter off with his arm around some woman. His mistresses adored him, because he was charismatic and powerfully built, as well as free with his money. My mother worked seven days a week as a seamstress to pay for our apartment and our food, because too often we had nothing from my father. In the end, she divorced him, and I had to live on a kibbutz. It was the worst year of my life, and I fantasized all the time that my father was going to come roaring up the dirt road in his Army jeep and take me off on a life of adventures.

He taught me to put order in my life. A career soldier, he believed in the value of discipline, perseverance, and self-confidence. Without those traits, I would never have enjoyed success. He taught me the importance of first impressions, too—he could walk into a restaurant and the room would fall silent, as if Cary Grant had made an entrance (though Cary Grant was never half so smooth and roguish as my father).

I'm grateful that he lived to see me enjoy international success. He died in 1979, and we'd long made our peace by then: It was not in our nature for either of us to bear grudges or carry anger. In those last years, he told me how bitterly he regretted that he had not been given an officer's commission, though he was ten times the soldier that most captains and majors could hope to be. He'd risen to the rank of five-star regimental sergeant major, and he'd taken his meals in the officers' mess . . . but he'd never been an officer, and that rankled.

I resolved then, back in the seventies, never to allow my ambitions to be thwarted. The energy and drive I've had in my later career has been fueled by my father's failures, as he saw them. But now that I'm the age that he was then, I know something else: Accept your achievements and celebrate your victories, however far short they have fallen of your dreams.

Phyllis George

A former Miss Texas and Miss America of 1971, Phyllis George has been a sportscaster and host for several shows, including CBS's The NFL Today. *She is the founder and CEO of Phyllis George Beauty, a beauty products company. She has also authored several books.*

"Bob Bob," as he was affectionately called by his grandchildren, was truly an amazing human being.

My father, Bob George, passed away several years ago. The lessons he taught me and my brother, Rob, and our children are invaluable. His spirit lives on with us every day in everything that we do.

I was born in Denton, Texas. My dad named me Phyllis Ann. We were a family that was rich in love. My parents were married for fifty years, and it was a true love affair. Dad wrote my mother, Louise, love letters up until the day he died.

When I was young, and throughout my life, he was always there comforting me, making me laugh, and

121

encouraging me. He always told me I was special and that I could accomplish anything, which gave me an enormous amount of confidence. Whenever times were tough, he had a sympathetic ear and a strong shoulder to lean on.

This churchgoing man who was an engineer by profession was a true southern gentleman. He spread his "light" to everyone with his big dimples, infectious smile, and charming personality, and was always upbeat with a great sense of humor. He was a caring and selfless man who put everyone else first. His greatest joy came from making others happy, and he left an impression on the heart of everyone he encountered.

The most important things my father taught me were the values of unconditional love and compassion for others. He treated everyone with the same respect and dignity, regardless of who they were.

He was appreciative of everything, and he taught me to always remember who I was and to never forget where I came from.

In fact, I remember a story very vividly from when I was in New Orleans covering the Super Bowl for CBS's *NFL Today*. Dad stopped by my room with some fatherly advice. While he was there, the housekeeper came to the door to see if I would like turndown service for the evening, to which he replied, "She can turn down her own bed, thank you very much."

I remember how my father stayed true to his beliefs

and never wavered. He never changed from day to day, which is why I feel my brother and I have the foundations we do today. While we might have veered at times, we always returned to our roots and what we were taught growing up. I think that speaks volumes. As I have grown older and now that he is gone, I reflect back and am so appreciative of what he left us and the positive impact he had on me and our family. I've tried to instill these same values in my own children, Lincoln and Pamela.

He was a loyal friend and never judgmental. He was also an adoring grandfather, a pretty good golfer, a fabulous dancer, and an amazing short-order cook. He was famous for his pancakes!

I adored my father and the lessons I learned from him. I was a daddy's girl—that's for sure.

David Gergen

David Gergen served as a White House adviser to Presidents Nixon, Ford, Reagan, and Clinton. He is currently a professor of public service at Harvard's John F. Kennedy School of Government and serves as editor at large for U.S. News & World Report.

When I was fifteen, I gloried in a job reporting on high school football games for our local newspaper in North Carolina, the *Durham Morning Herald.* I was too young to drive, so on Friday nights, my dad would take me to games and then to the newspaper office at around ten o'clock, where I would hunt and peck my way through a story and usually finish well past the midnight deadline. What always stirred me was that Dad would sit outside in the family Chevy, hour after hour, smoking and patiently waiting until I finished so he could drive me home . . . or perhaps to a party. He didn't have to do that, but he did, and I have never forgotten.

Cancer took Dad at a cruelly early age, sixty-three, almost four decades ago. But a day rarely passes when I don't think of him and thank him for his steadfast, generous, loving support during my growing-up years. He could be gruff—boy, could he—and I sometimes rebelled under his demanding eye. What I remember now, though, are the countless scenes where he would be there for me. Playing catcher on Sundays after church as I tried (vainly) to become a better pitcher. Sitting up waiting into the wee hours Saturday night, when I could finally drive and straggled home from dates. Urging me to apply to Andover but secretly pleased when I turned down my acceptance in order to stay home. Inviting me to join the conversation as he and my sainted mother sat for their regular nightcap before bed. Taking a second job, putting in incredible hours, so he could pay my way through college and law school. Drilling me at the blackboard over college breaks when I was spending so much time with the college newspaper that I was nearly flunking calculus. He was math chairman at Duke for a quarter century and told me early on that unless you're very, very good at a subject like math, go elsewhere—sound advice.

Dad was sometimes harder on my three older brothers. By the time I came along, the tadpole, he had mellowed a bit and was easier on me. But he taught all of us how to be there—how to care, how to support, how to give intense, unconditional love. I sometimes worry that I have not been as good with my own two kids as he was with me; fortunately, my wife filled in during my many absences when they were toddlers and I was trying to climb the slippery pole in Washington. But as they have grown older, married, and begun to have children of their own, I have tried to be there more for them, always holding up my dad as my model. In almost every thing I do today—from personal to professional—his imprint remains profound. I always miss him.

Newt Gingrich

Elected to the House of Representatives in November 1978, Newt Gingrich was reelected ten more times. Named Time *magazine's Man of the Year in 1995, Newt Gingrich is best known for serving as Speaker of the House from 1995 to 1999.*

Thinking about the key influences in my life made me realize that I had three strong, unique men who taught me about life. I am adopted, and my stepfather, Bob Gingrich, played a decisive role in shaping my life. However, my father, Newt McPherson, also taught me a lot. Finally, I could not describe men who influenced me without mentioning my uncle, Cal Troutman, who helped raise me and taught me so much.

First, it was Bob Gingrich, who as an infantry officer in the U.S. Army got me to realize how dangerous the world is and how badly America needs leadership to remain free and safe. It was while we were stationed in Orleans, France, in 1958 (I was fifteen at the time) that we visited the battlefield of Verdun and stayed with a friend who had been drafted in 1941, sent to the Philippines, suffered on the Bataan death march, and survived three and a half years in a Japanese prison camp. It was in the process of visiting the largest battlefield on the western front in World War I and then listening to stories about life in a prison camp that I began to realize how real the threats were for my parents' generation and for my country. That summer, between my freshman and sophomore years in high school, I gave up my dreams of being either a vertebrate paleontologist or a zoo director and decided that trying to help my country remain free and safe was my vocation as a citizen. Forty-seven years later, I am still on the path launched by that weekend.

Second, Newt McPherson was a strong individual in the John Wayne tradition. He believed that you had to respect others and you had to insist that they respect you. He had a deep love of life and a great sense of humor. He taught me what I learned years later was the rule Fox Conner had taught Dwight D. Eisenhower, then a major: "You should always take your job seriously and never yourself." In many ways, my entire approach to working hard but enjoying life and focusing on the duty to be done and not on personal aggrandizement came from his lessons.

Third, my uncle Cal was a very small man but very strong. He had worked as a young man in a slaughterhouse and could carry a side of beef on his shoulder (this was before automation). He had grown up in a very tough neighborhood. Once he was shot as a young man. When he was telling the story, I asked, awestruck, "What did you do?" He said, with a grin, "I chased the guy, but I couldn't run very fast with a bullet in my leg and he got away." He said it was only a .22 bullet, but for a young guy that was still very impressive. He read Louis L'Amour Westerns and instilled in me a love of the American code of honesty, directness, and firmness.

All three men insisted on integrity, on a deep sense of patriotic belief in America, on a willingness to stand for what was right and fight for it if necessary. Together, they shaped me in ways that will be with me as long as I live.

Ira Glass

Ira Glass has worked in public radio broadcasting for more than twenty years. He is the host and producer of This American Life, *a journalistic nonfiction program that focuses on a particular thought-provoking social theme each week. The show is now distributed by Public Radio International and is heard by an estimated 1.7 million listeners on five hundred public radio stations each week.*

My dad, like a lot of men, wasn't the most talkative kind of person. If anything, a lot of the skills I've developed as a radio interviewer come from being in the car with him and trying to actually get him to speak about something, anything. Which I guess happens a lot. Kids develop personalities that are designed to fit into the jigsaw pieces of what their parents aren't.

I do remember the day my dad taught me how to shave. To be instructed by him about anything was so unusual that even as we stood there at the sink, I thought I'd remember it. Or maybe it was the boy-becomes-a-man symbolism of the moment that made it stand out. I was intensely aware of that, even at the time. It seemed a very significant thing for a dad to teach his son, and I wanted it to *mean* something. Which is probably why I still think about that day sometimes when I go to shave, three decades later. I can recall every part of his instructions: He explained that I had to wet my face down with hot water to soften the barely existent whiskers (which at the time seemed like such a strange thing to say that I wondered if he knew what he was talking about), and showed me how to hold the razor and the length of the strokes. When it came to the actual shaving, he realized he needed to stand behind me and reach up to my face at the same angle that he was used to shaving his own. He stood close to me when he did this, which was also unusual. He was a conscientious dad, a worried dad, a caring dad, but not so big on the physical contact.

What stands out most about this memory is how few memories I have that are like this: of him actually teaching me something, or taking the time to impart some kind of lesson about the world.

I can tie my shoes, I can drive, I can balance a checkbook, I can throw a football in a spiral. I know he had a hand in all that. But to get this kind of focused attention from him was rare. His father left his mother when Dad was five, and I guess he just never saw any man spend time with a boy this way. It never occurred to him it was something he might try more often.

Instead, I ended up taking a lot of lessons from him

that he never said anything about but that just kind of seeped into me. For instance, he was incredibly scrupulous in business, which is something I just take for granted in my own business dealings. But when I try to think about why I wouldn't cut corners, or practice the everyday kinds of hyperaggressive, dog-eat-dog tactics that exist in every kind of business (even the nicey-nicey world of public broadcasting), I can't remember him ever trying to explain any principles of how to act or anything like that. Instead, I remember offhand comments he made about his clients. These were as infrequent as passing comets; he was a very discreet man. Someone would really have to piss him off to get mentioned in front of his kids. But I'd examine every utterance about his job for guideposts to his thinking. As a CPA, he ran across a lot of people who'd cut corners in business. He didn't abide that. He shook his head wearily at people who spent more than they made, and had no respect for businesses that had a lot of cash flow but made no profit ("Anybody can do volume," he said once; "the trick is to make money"). He didn't offer these insights for me and my sisters to learn from; they were simply in the air in our house, and we breathed them in.

In the end, I think most of what we learn from our parents they never intended for us to learn anyway. This stuff just shows up inside us, like a virus that they never intended to transmit and we didn't intend to catch.

Governor Jennifer Granholm

Originally from Vancouver, British Columbia, Jennifer Gran-holm became a U.S. citizen at the age of twenty-one. After serving as Michigan's attorney general for four years, she was sworn in as that state's first female governor on January 1, 2003.

My dad, Victor, is the most humble, gentle man I've ever met. He has taught me so many valuable lessons over the years, but the one that has stuck with me the most is to always be honest and positive. He taught this lesson by example. He is an early riser, toiling when he worked as a banker from 5 a.m. until he arrived home after 7 p.m.

He never complains, never speaks ill of others, and never curses. His discomfort is visible when he hears negative gossip, and he always steers the conversation to the best in people. He never lifts himself by pushing others down.

Perhaps most endearing is his great belly laugh when my irreverent mom tells a joke. In this, he taught me an equally important and valuable lesson—to love and enjoy my spouse in things big and small.

Lisa Graves

As senior counsel for legislative strategy for the American Civil Liberties Union, Lisa Graves works primarily on national security issues. During the Clinton administration, she was one of the youngest people to be promoted to a career post as deputy assistant attorney general at the U.S. Department of Justice.

I've been fortunate enough to serve as a senior adviser in all three branches of the federal government and now as the senior lobbyist for the American Civil Liberties Union on national security issues. But more than that, I've been fortunate enough to have a father whose persistence and determination have made my professional success and happiness not just a possibility but a concrete reality.

When I was ten years old, my father, Richard Graves, returned to our home outside of Denver after the surgery to save his vision failed. Within months, he would go from seeing only shadows in bright sunlight to "seeing" only darkness. It was a terribly sad time in our house—he was only twenty-nine, a young man who had simple pleasures, like restoring antique cars, who savored his freedom, his ability to hop on his beloved motorcycle and race down mountain roads with the wind in his hair and not a care in the world.

My dad had already lost his vision in one eye the

year before I was born in a construction accident—a wire had struck him in the eye, and there was no way to repair the damage. He did not let this deter him. He had volunteered to go to Vietnam, but was not allowed to serve because of his physical condition. An impulsive young man, he had actually dropped out of high school after his gym teacher teased him relentlessly about his thick glasses, but he knew he wanted to spend his life working on cars and didn't think he needed a high school diploma for that.

In the years before he lost the sight in his "good" eye, he demonstrated time and again his independence and determination. He had trouble securing a job as a mechanic due to his monocular vision, and refused to apply for any welfare from the state. I remember thinking as a kid how fun my dad's odd jobs were, but I never, not once, heard him complain about them, and I didn't learn until much later that these jobs were considered undesirable—they barely paid a living wage. While he looked for a permanent job as an auto mechanic, my dad ran roller coasters at Lakeside Amusement Park; he was a cook at Wyatt's cafeteria (his specialty was a delicious chicken-fried steak); at one point, he had three paper routes delivering the *Rocky Mountain News* (during third grade, I must have put thousands of comic sections into many thousands of papers in the wee hours of the morning with him); and he "shagged" cars, washing and waxing them for car dealerships, just trying to show his work ethic and to get his foot in the door to be hired as a mechanic.

I remember when he finally got his dream job working as a mechanic. There was almost no task he loved more than rolling up his sleeves and solving some mechanical mystery or just fixing a tire. I remember Sunday afternoons when he was not at work, spending the day with him working on the 1960 Lincoln Continental convertible he was trying to restore. I remember long drives to the mountains on his motorcycle or in his convertible with the radio blasting and the top down. When I sometimes complained about the summer heat, he'd say we had "255 AC"—that is, two windows down at fifty-five miles per hour. While my dad was by no means perfect, I can honestly say I never heard him complain about his jobs, his loss of his left eye, or his lot in life.

Even after he lost his sight completely, I remember my parents arguing about how they could pay the mortgage or buy food, but I always remember that giving up was never an option. After he was completely blind, my father went back to get another degree in auto repair. At the time, I knew it was quite a feat to earn a degree in auto mechanics as a totally blind person, but it was only after I was older and in law school that I genuinely realized the incredible feat it was when I described for my new friends how, at age eleven, I watched my dad rebuild piece by piece an entire automatic transmission without being able to see a thing.

Once my dad starts a project, there is no way to talk him out of it. While we were learning Braille together at night, by day he would still be doing things dads and kids take for granted—from sharpening the blades of our push mower to fixing the garbage disposal or riding a tandem bike with me—all the while unable to see my face or his own hand even in the strongest summer sun.

After my dad got his second mechanics degree, he went back to car companies to get a job, but discrimination was rampant. Even though he had earned his degree without any sight, people didn't want to hire a blind mechanic. Anyone who has worked on cars, however, knows that a lot of what you do is by "feel" and a lot of diagnosis is by sound. In the 1970s and '80s, before computers were installed in cars, the only thing my dad needed was some quick advice on electrical wiring—to make sure he had the right colored wire mentioned in the repair books that he practically knew by heart from when he could see.

The discrimination was really heartbreaking for him, and when he finally did complain to the state of Colorado, they suggested that he should join the other people with disabilities at the broomstick factory. I know the sheer repetition of the job would have driven such a creative and mechanically oriented man like my dad crazy. Instead, he embarked on another series of unusual ventures, some of which we argued about quite a bit. But when my brother was born nineteen years ago, my dad decided to become the homemaker in our house and settle down. My dad and I certainly have had some rough patches—because I absorbed his independence and his determination through to my very bones—but I honestly learned so much through his toils and triumphs that I would not ask for a different dad, even if such a thing were possible.

To this day, when one of our cars has trouble, my dad just embraces it as an opportunity to solve a problem! His determination is a living example to me to never give up, to embrace obstacles as opportunities, to believe almost anything is possible, and to defy the limits people might place on your potential.

I have used these lessons throughout my life. As a college student, I wanted to work at a law firm, but I had no experience. On his advice, I opened a phone book and started applying in person at the top of the list, at the *A*s. I got my start in the legal profession when one of the firms in the *B*s decided to take a risk and give me a job as a law clerk.

When I was applying to law school, I decided to try to get into an Ivy League school, even though I attended a state school at a satellite campus—not the most prestigious college, but one with excellent and devoted professors. Cornell Law School accepted me, and I went on to become the managing editor of the *Law Review*, graduating with honors.

In the Clinton administration, I was chosen to join the Attorney General's Honor Program as a new attorney. Frustrated with my job litigating policy decisions I often disagreed with, I decided to apply for my dream job of making policy at the Justice Department. Competing against Rhodes scholars and others with fantastic pedigrees, I got the job, and within two years was promoted to be deputy assistant attorney general, one of the youngest career appointees ever given this position. In that role, I wrote speeches for the attorney general and tackled numerous projects that were seen as daunting. Relying on the lessons my father taught me, I remember thinking each time, "We can do it!"

After I left the Justice Department and also my senior leadership role with the U.S. courts, I joined Senator Patrick Leahy as his chief nominations counsel. People told me the Democrats would never stand up to the president and his coveted judicial nominees, even if they were extremists. I knew some of them were chosen not to be fair judges but to be sure things in decisions against civil rights and civil liberties claims. In reviewing a record, I would often consider whether the nominee would give a fair shake to ordinary people like my parents, or whether they would prejudge the case to advance some partisan, political agenda. To me, the most important trait of a judge is fairness—we all know smart, judgmental people who should not be trusted with the power to decide others' fates.

When people would say that a particular nominee couldn't be beat, I would counter that anything was possible, and if it was the right thing to protect our Constitution, we should make the best case we could. We did, and in my opinion we stopped ten of the worst nominees from getting lifetime jobs deciding cases that affect our health, our wealth, and our daily lives. Even in my current role as the senior lobbyist on national security and civil liberties issues for the American Civil Liberties Union, this determination and optimism animates my work in building a coalition across the political spectrum to protect both our security and our legacy of liberty as Americans.

Robert F. Kennedy once said, "Some people see things as they are and ask why. I dream of things that never were and ask why not." My dad was never attorney general, but he shares this fundamental philosophy. My father is neither rich nor famous, but his lessons to me are priceless and enduring. And I know I am blessed that through his blindness he gave me a shining light to live my life by: Never give up! Anything is possible!

J. B. Handelsman

J. B. Handelsman's work has regularly appeared in The
New Yorker *and* Playboy. *An internationally recognized cartoonist, he has illustrated numerous books, including* Families and How to Survive Them, Life and How to Survive
It, *and* The Mid-Atlantic Companion.

My father was one of the most honest and upright
people I have ever known—and he may have inherited this trait from *his* father, who once traveled a
long distance to return five cents he had accidentally
overcharged someone. This was so unusual that it was
reported in the *New York World.*

My father never gave me advice, apart from urging
me to wear warm clothes in winter. I'm grateful for
that; I always made my own decisions, and some of
them were foolish, but they were mine! I seldom give
advice to my own children, and perhaps some day
they will thank me for that. Or perhaps not . . .

R. M. Dolores Hart, Pr., O.S.B.

*After a successful career as a Broadway and film star,
Dolores Hart left Hollywood at the age of twenty-five to become a Roman Catholic nun. Today, the reverend mother is*

the only nun to be an Oscar-voting member of the Academy of Motion Picture Arts and Sciences.

When I was six years old, my father and mother were divorcing, and I was sent to live with my grandparents in Chicago. I wasn't too happy about the arrangement. I didn't know that it was going to be one of the happiest times of my life.

Grandma Kude was especially good to me. She was both loving and strict. She taught me to wash and iron and clean house, and to knit and crochet (I could hand stitch anything by the time I was ten); showed me how to brush and set my hair; and helped me to learn to read by reading to me—every one of the Oz books.

But if Grandma was my best friend, Grandpa was my best buddy and the closest I ever came to having a real father. Grandpa was German and worked as a projectionist at the Drake movie house in Chicago. He used to take me with him up to the projection booth on weekends, where I would see all the movies through the little projection window. There wasn't, however, any sound except Grandpa's voice talking back to the actors on the screen, sometimes in German. Whenever he would be particularly displeased with them, or me, or even with himself, he would say, *"Gott, ich bin ein dummer Esel. Schlag mich auf den Kopf und mach' mich wieder klug."* I didn't know exactly what it meant, but it sounded a little like a prayer, and it seemed to make him feel better. The words became part of my memory of him.

Grandpa got me my first job—at age seven—washing tombstones at the cemetery behind our duplex. I got a nickel a marker, and when I earned $2 I bought a Tinkertoy set. Grandpa was a mechanical mastermind and had a workshop in our basement where I'd stand for hours watching him put together the most wonderful contraptions. He motorized everything, including my Tinkertoys. Anything I could build out of them he could make run. Together we built a Ferris wheel that actually worked. We once made a series of tiny parachutes that we mounted on a huge kite, and when the kite was aloft, he was able to release them one by one. I put our telephone number in each parachute and was forever hopeful that we would get a call from whoever found one of them. But we never did.

He taught me how to use all the tools in his toolbox and to respect them. He also taught me to take pride in building things and repairing them. It seems, when I was growing up, that I was always in sweatshirts and blue jeans, tinkering with this and that. I could take bikes apart and put them together again. I'd get on the roof and help fix the TV antenna. I became the Miss Fix-It of the family.

In 1963, I entered Regina Laudis in Bethlehem, Connecticut, a monastery of contemplative women living in union with the Roman Catholic Church and following the Rule of St. Benedict according to the Primitive Observance. The dynamic character of our monastic life is explained in three words: prayer, study, and work.

Early in my monastic life, a noted artist came to the monastery to give lessons in portraiture. I studied with this gifted woman for several months, and one day she said, "Sister, you have wonderful energy. I think you should do something that would really help the community." She was being sweetly diplomatic, but it gave me an idea. Why not let Grandpa take over?

I became the community's carpenter and handyperson. A professional carpenter from nearby Woodbury taught me how to work with wood. We slowly acquired some excellent equipment—a table saw and a joiner—and I began building shelves, monastic tables, small desks (and coffins) for the community. I found it deeply gratifying work, especially in a time when craftsmanship has been replaced by manufactured things with little soul or style. I feel I had a real call to bring to woodwork a quality I was also taught to respect when I was an actress, by the masters I worked with such as Anna Magnani, Anthony Quinn, Robert Ryan, Myrna Loy, Cyril Ritchard, Cornelia Otis Skinner, and Karl Malden.

And whenever I felt I produced something of lesser quality than I wanted, I thought of Grandpa's words: *"Gott, ich bin ein dummer Esel. Schlag mich auf den Kopf und mach' mich wieder klug."*

God, I am a dumb ass. Hit me over the head and make me smart again.

Patricia Heaton

An Emmy Award–winning television and film actress, Patricia Heaton is best known for her starring role on the long-running hit show Everybody Loves Raymond.

M y dad worried about money. A lot. He had five kids in parochial school, a mortgage, and a great but not high-paying job as a sportswriter for the *Cleveland Plain Dealer*. His job afforded him a bunch of perks, like free tickets to anything at the Coliseum (the suffering he endured every year at the Ice Capades was payment enough!), so we always felt pretty flush. But the reality was that he had to work hard under grueling deadlines to keep me in Mary Janes.

Nevertheless, my clearest memory of Chuck Heaton is him sitting at the dining room table, glasses on his nose, checkbook in hand, surrounded by bills—writing checks to the Maryknoll missions and Father Flanagan's Boys Town. He was always ready to help anyone in need, and faithfully gave of what was given to him. He really took the message of Christ to heart: "Whatever you do to the least of these, you do to me."

My dad is quite elderly now, and is really struggling physically. He often asks me, in his quavering voice, if I think he will get into heaven. I think God's clearest memory of my dad will be the same as mine—looking after the least of God's children.

Steven Hill

A founding member of Lee Strasberg's Actors Studio, Steven Hill has had a long and distinguished stage, film, and television career, including prominent roles in such landmark series as Law & Order *and* Mission: Impossible.

My father, may he rest in peace, was a giant of a man. He was able to see through to the essence of things, and of people. He had a habit of defining what he saw with one word or a very short phrase.

We took a walk one day in Palm Springs, where my father and mother would spend the winters in their later years. We came to a place where there were a few trees filled with, it seemed, hundreds of birds, chirping away and carrying on nonstop. "Dad," I asked, "what do you think the birds are saying?" He answered, "Where's the food?"

He started his working life at the age of twelve, as a night watchman on a farm in czarist Russia. He must have been mature enough even at that age to shoulder responsibility. Later, he employed his two brothers from Russia in the furniture store he established in Seattle, the People's Furniture Company, and brought over his mother as well. His name was Hillel Krakovsky. People in Seattle called him "Mr. Hill."

I grew up in my father's house, along with my brother and two sisters, always feeling I would never get to know him. He never talked that much about himself, or others. But he could tell the difference between the hot air and the genuine.

The chief principles he taught us to live by were:

"The best thing for a man is silence."
"Everything in due time."
"Learn to read between the lines."
"Don't get a swelled head."
"Obey the law."
And on important decisions, "Sleep on it" (overnight).

His strength of character and sense of fair play were deeply rooted in his personality—yet with flashes of a brilliant sense of humor when he chose to let go.

He is a hard act to follow. But in these later years, I have tried to fashion most of my acting work in his image when the situation and mood appropriately presents itself.

He was a genuine article.

Marty Ingels

An actor-comedian whose films include If It's Tuesday, This Must Be Belgium *and* A Guide for the Married Man, *Marty Ingels has been married to actress-singer Shirley Jones since 1977.*

I wrote this piece not because I thought anyone would ever print it, but because I thought it'd be good therapy for me when someone asked, "What lessons did you learn from your father?" Nobody ever asked me that before. It was time to stand up and spit it out or forever hold my peace.

The fact is that if I learned anything from my honest, uneducated, bighearted, unambitious, fun-loving, noncompetitive, Russian-born and Brooklyn-settled, couldn't-make-a-living-for-the-life-of-him, too-good, too-soft, and too-generous ol' man, it was that honest, soft, generous, good-hearted guys come in last. That's what my father did till his dying day.

And that's because he never made it in the savvy-status-achievement department. So he came in last, everywhere. And all those other beautiful human things poets rhapsodize about were lost to a society that looks to the marketplace for its heroes. Oh sure, today . . . the family, the grown-up kids, sit around and savor the touching, tender memories of "Uncle Jack." Above all, the movers and shakers we had in our nest (including a mayor of New York), they go down the old familiar "Uncle Jack List" again: "warm" and "funny" and "gentle." And the truth? I get mad. I just get *mad*. Where was this gushing Nobel Prize committee when Mr. Goodwrench was *alive?* There was no applause then, not for the hapless auto mechanic who couldn't make the family bills most of the time. No fan clubs then, or support groups. It was only "poor Jack."

It even trickled down to us, his own kids. And it shouldn't have. He should've been Batman and Superman to us, no matter what he earned. But he wasn't. He was a sweet, easy, good-time loser.

My more idealistic wife dramatically disagrees with me on this one. She contends that he, my father, had the ultimate gift. You know, that "pure," "proud," "spiritual" rap. "Inheritors of the earth" and all that. And I say, "Poppycock" (and some other words you won't let me say). My father had some of the goods at the PTA and none at the BOA—period.

Now, I blame nothing and no one for my father's lowly social station. As for the impatience I feel for the Monday-morning cheerleaders who gather and dribble around—well, I'm not really sure I understand that. Maybe it's part of the general anger I've come to know I feel toward him, angel that he was, for letting them swarm over and devour him, for not putting up more of a fight, and, finally, for checking out too early and too quickly just when my glory boat was so close to home.

So, now that you know him, you ask, "What lessons did you learn from your father?" My answer is that I learned only one thing—not by any one-to-one "teaching" my father would have loved to have imparted, but by the graphic, living scenario the ubiquitous world bolted around my father every day during all those early years when I sat there and watched. I learned the practical lesson of life in America, maybe the world:

Be good and warm and sweet and generous and all those other Hallmark favorites my father was, but be them second, next, as a backup, in the wings, on hold, in the trunk, at your cousin's (if at all)!

First, be successful. First, be accomplished. Find something you do better than anyone else and first, be a winner. First, be all those Dow Jones things my father wasn't.

You'd be amazed at how everything else will fall into place. That's the way it came down for me.

Victoria Jackson

After twenty-two appearances on The Tonight Show *with Johnny Carson, Victoria Jackson starred in numerous movies and television shows. She is perhaps best known for her six seasons as a cast member of* Saturday Night Live.

He was tan and muscular, though always struggling with his little pooch of a stomach. He wore a hat, a whistle around his neck, and thick, white, greasy stuff on his nose. He was my elementary school phys. ed. teacher. He got so happy when a student threw the softball two feet farther than he did last year. He was elated when a chubby kid did her first pull-up on the bar. If a kid said a curse word, he'd make the kid write it on a slip of paper, sign it, and take it home for his parents to sign. Many times the parents would call my dad at home and curse at him.

On the playing field, he taught us to be good losers. "Always shake hands with the winner and congratulate them." Never say the word "cheat." Never lie. "Stealing and lying are the same thing," he would say. He always treated the girls equally with the boys on the athletic field, maybe because he was also a women's gymnastics coach by night. Gymnastics was his passion. This dedication toward physical perfection started when he turned his own chubby high school body into the University of Chicago's star athlete. His sudden source of self-esteem amazed him, and he shared this passion with thousands of students throughout his coaching life.

His imagination turned our childhood into a wonderland. He designed homemade costumes and props for his circuses and tumbling shows. At Camp Ocala, he buried himself alive under four feet of dirt trying to top the previous year's campfire show. He dressed up my brother and me as Indians and made us do back-flips off a trampoline through a real fire. Forget Hollywood studios—my dad was the writer, director, trainer, makeup artist, costumer, and star of all of his productions. The parents in our lower-middle-class neighborhood were enthralled with his shows. We had no TV. It would interfere with our afternoon workouts. There was a balance beam, parallel bars, and a sunken trampoline in our hot, humid Florida backyard.

Every Sunday, our family was at church in the third row. Dad taught Sunday school. He could answer any question on the Bible and would whip out his thirty or so reference books if he ever got stumped. He also read the Koran, the Book of Mormon, the *Watchtower*, and L. Ron Hubbard's *Dianetics* just to make sure his faith was the right one. He played the piano every night. While I did my homework in my room, I subliminally fell in love with Gershwin, Cole Porter, Rodgers and Hart. He taught us how to harmonize, tap dance, water-ski, and read before we went to school so we'd be ahead of the class. He put a chin-up bar in my brother's doorway and told him to do a pull-up every time he entered or exited his room. I learned what a vision was. I learned that if you do fifty sit-ups every day, you will be able to do a glide kip on the bars in a year, and maybe win the gym meet in two years.

Dad only took us to clean movies. He said that whatever you see will stick in your head forever. My dad worked three or four jobs, never missed a day of work, and was happy all the time. My dad never had a drink or a cigarette, never cheated on my mom or told a dirty joke. My dad is still teaching gymnastics at the age of seventy-six, after four hip replacement surgeries and skin cancer. He never complains or raises his voice. And when we all hold hands at the dinner table and he prays, I can feel God in the room. Dad taught me that life counts, every moment of it.

Derek Jeter

Derek Jeter was named the eleventh captain in New York Yankees history in June 2003. In 2000, he became the first player in baseball history to be named the most valuable player in the All-Star Game and World Series in the same season. A six-time all-star, he was the American League rookie of the year in 1996.

You learn a lot of lessons. I don't know if I can really give you one. There are a lot of things that a father teaches you growing up, lessons that at the time you may not agree with or understand. You always make mistakes as a kid, and I think your job as a parent is to point those things out. There've been plenty of times that's happened. I remember losing a game one time when I was younger, playing baseball on a Little League team, and I didn't shake hands with the other team. My dad told me that if I wanted to be like that, I should play an individual sport. From then, I was always the first one to shake hands.

Randy Johnson

A five-time Cy Young Award winner, Randy Johnson has led Major League Baseball in strikeouts nine times in his career; his six 300-strikeout seasons are the most ever. In May 2004, he recorded the fifteenth perfect game in modern-day regular-season history. He is the fourth member of the four-thousand-strikeout club and has struck out more batters than any other left-handed pitcher.

My dad tried to instill in me that when you do something, you should do it to the best of your ability the first time because you may not have a second opportunity to do it. It was about anything you did, even if it was a chore around the house when I was younger. But it carried over into my profession. So when you do something, it has your name on it. You may not always be successful in what you do, but when you do it, do it to the best of your ability.

Jack Klugman

An award-winning film, television, and Broadway actor,
Jack Klugman is recognized as one of the pioneers of 1950s
television and has starred in several series, including The
Odd Couple *and* Quincy, M.E.

I am the youngest of a large family—I had four brothers and one older sister. My father was a carefree man who had a full head of uncombed gray hair and a full tobacco-stained mustache. He had strong features, and yet he seemed vulnerable. He died when I was only twelve years old, and that made me very angry. I felt that he had abandoned me. At that age, I didn't really know what death was. If I wished someone dead, it was because I wanted them gone temporarily so they wouldn't be able to say no to whatever it was I wanted to do. I really mourned his death twenty years after he died. I was on a psychiatrist's couch. I wept so hard that he had to keep me in his office an extra hour. No, he did not charge me for that extra hour.

It was then that I remembered that my father was the only one in my family that ever hugged me. The rest of my family stayed away from any touching or hugging—especially my mother. My brothers would offer a stiff handshake to ward off any hugs, and my sister didn't know what an embrace was until she got married at the age of forty-five!

My mother was a wonderful, strong, hardworking woman, but no one comes into this world without some baggage. She received no love from her parents and passed that legacy on to us. She gave us a lot of protection but no love.

Only my father was unashamed to show affection. He would rub his unshaven chin against my young face and we both would laugh uncontrollably. It felt like I was being tickled, so I would squirm and giggle and he would laugh at my reaction. I remember feeling so happy after one of those tickles.

You know, as we grow old (I'm eighty-three) we become a bag of memories, and if we are lucky, as I am, the bad memories fall through the loosely knitted burlap and all that remains are the good memories.

My father taught me that showing your affection was not a sign of weakness but instead a sign of love. I have passed his legacy on to my two sons and my granddaughters. Whenever I see them, we kiss and hug and show how fond we are of each other. I love it!

And I thank my father for his legacy every time I walk past his picture in my home.

C. Everett Koop, M.D., Sc.D.

Born in Brooklyn, New York, C. Everett Koop served as surgeon-in-chief at the Children's Hospital of Pennsylvania

*before becoming surgeon general in 1982. During his seven
years of service, he was an outspoken advocate of public-
health issues and transformed the office of surgeon general into one of the most prominent positions in the U.S.
government.*

My father was not only my father, but also my best
friend. I learned at his funeral from one of his
secretaries (of many years earlier) that he considered
no question that I asked him too big or too small to deserve an answer. When I had asked a zinger for which
he did not know the answer, it was his custom to take
his lunch hour the next day and spend it at the New
York Public Library at Forty-second Street and Fifth
Avenue finding the answer. I remember many of the
nights he came home for dinner and said something
like "You remember last night we were talking about
so-and-so and you asked me . . . well, here's the answer. Let me draw you a picture to make it clear."

My family owned its first automobile when I turned
eight or nine. It was a spiffy little Jordan of pearl-gray—
a color remarkable in itself in those days—and my
father taught me to drive it in Nova Scotia when I was
ten. The year before we owned a car, my father and I
were walking briskly to some destination to which we
would have driven had we owned a car. It was then
that I asked my father, "Dad, why don't we have a car?"

He replied, "Son, I could buy almost any car you

see driving by us, but I really can't afford to buy one. By that, I mean I would rather protect you and your mother financially if I should die, or, better yet, have the necessary funds to put you through college and medical school. I spend my money on things I think are more important to us at this time of our lives than a car."

"But Uncle Clarence and Uncle Victor both have big cars. What about them?"

"Well. They certainly bought their cars, but just between you and me, I don't really think they could afford them."

It was not until two years later that I learned that my two uncles had purchased their cars with money they borrowed from my father. Meanwhile, he continued to protect the family, which worked out just fine. We also had a car.

His explanation of the difference between "afford" and "buy" has been an economic guide for me ever since.

Pat LaFontaine

Former hockey star Pat LaFontaine was a member of the 1984 and 1998 U.S. Olympic teams, and played fifteen seasons in the National Hockey League for the New York Islanders, Buffalo Sabres, and New York Rangers. He was elected to the Hockey Hall of Fame in 2003.

On the day of my fifteenth birthday, the U.S. hockey team upset the Russians in the "Miracle" game at Lake Placid. (I believe there are no coincidences in life.) For the first time in my life, I thought there might be a glimmer of hope for an American kid to make it to the National Hockey League.

My father, John, had been a coach for my brother and me in youth hockey leagues around Michigan. He always stressed that we should continue to develop our strengths, but we should also pay particular attention to our weaknesses. He reasoned that human nature caused people to gravitate toward and rely on things they did well. Consequently, they tend to try to hide their weakest skills. If your opponent is able to discover those weaknesses, you'll be exploited until you ultimately fail.

Growing up, my brother and I played hockey for hours on Williams Lake, behind our house in Michigan. My sister would be practicing her figure skating, while Mom brought the hot chocolate and the advice to "get in from the cold." We had a lot of fun, but my dad always made me work on my skating and passing, while my brother spent a lot of extra time on his shot. If we were ever to have a chance at a college scholarship or the pros, Dad knew we needed to excel in these areas where we may have been weak.

My dad's logic makes sense whether you're applying it to academics, sports, or business. In order to develop as the most well-rounded person you can be, you cannot rely solely on your strengths. My dad was an executive in the Lee Iacocca regime at the Chrysler Corporation. He was the guy who would be brought in to help fix "broken" plants. As his son, I could see how he was able to navigate that bumpy road to productivity.

He is a man of tremendous character and dignity. On the ice, I admired the play of Guy Lafleur and Gilbert Perreault. But in life, my dad always served as my role model. He taught me how to treat people by respecting myself first, and then looking for the good that we all possess. I suppose one of the reasons I started the Companions in Courage Foundation to help sick kids in children's hospitals was based on the values I learned from my dad. He taught his kids that if you were ever in a position to help those less fortunate, it was your moral obligation to do so.

As a kid, my dad made us value everything we ever earned. If I wanted a new pair of skates, I had to caddy for weeks to earn the money to buy them. If I needed a new stick, I cleaned out the stalls in our local hockey rink to earn the money to buy it. You never got something for nothing in our house. It made me appreciate everything that was dear to me.

I guess one of the greatest gifts a father can give a son is the example of how to treat your wife. My parents had their share of disagreements, as any couple married for more than forty years would have. But he always treated my mother with the utmost respect. It was obvious how much he loved her by the caring way he spoke to her and consulted her on big decisions.

In the summer of 2004, my mom finally succumbed to a lifetime of illness and complications from heart disease. The loss of his lifetime love is one of the hardest things for any man to deal with. But I watched as my dad helped Mom pass on with dignity and the most tender care.

Even though I'm grown with a family of my own, my dad continues to be a source of inspiration, education, and strength. And, oh yeah, he still inspires me to work on my weaknesses.

Jack LaLanne

An internationally recognized fitness, exercise, and nutritional expert, Jack LaLanne opened the first gym in the United States and is known as the "father of fitness." A recipient of the Horatio Alger Association of Distinguished Americans Horatio Alger Award, he continues to work out every day for two hours.

I loved my father very dearly but, unfortunately, the life lessons I learned from him took a very sad turn at an early age for me. It was during the Depression and my dad, Jean (Jon) LaLanne, was a very hardworking man who lived by the slogan "I never told my stomach I'm a poor man." He loved to eat and indulge himself with the worst diet imaginable. My father's big hobby was shopping for food. His favorite foods were cheese, meat, and butter. This resulted in a very unhealthy lifestyle. I literally watched my father take his own life with his knife and fork.

Early in my life, both of my parents were afflicted by various ailments and, as a child, I was a sugarholic and sick all the time. I was an adolescent junk-food junkie. I had boils and pimples and needed arch supports and glasses. I frequently had blinding headaches so bad I used to pound my head against the wall because I couldn't stop the pain. I was getting failing grades in school. At that point in my life, I didn't care to live anymore. Finally, I had to drop out of school for six months, due to ill health. It was during this time that a neighbor suggested that my mother take me to a health lecture in Oakland, California. I didn't want to go, but my mother dragged me along.

That lecture, by pioneer nutritionist Paul Bragg, became a turning point in my life. He said that I could be reborn, meaning that if I were to obey nature's laws, improve my eating habits, and take up an exercise program, I could change my body. I immediately stopped eating white flour and sugar products, ate foods in their natural state as often as possible, and joined the local YMCA. I was inspired! My goal was to have a healthy body, play sports, and be a good student. I bought a copy of *Gray's Anatomy* and read it cover to cover. I went back to school, became captain of the football team and an AAU wrestling champion in my weight class for the state of California, sold dates and nuts on the side as a part-time job, and preached nutrition to my classmates. I also set up a gym in my backyard. I built exercise equipment of my own invention.

Although my dad's work ethic was strong and I know how much of my mental strength came from observing his mental toughness, he was an unconscious victim of his own dietary overindulgence. I am convinced that the excessive amounts of fat from the meats and cheeses he consumed daily contributed to his early passing. He didn't go along with my philosophies. I'd say to him, "Dad, come exercise with me." He'd reply, "Aw, kid, that exercise is just for you young kids." Then he would have a second helping of mashed potatoes loaded with melted butter and gravy made from animal fat. I tried in vain to get him to change his eating habits, but he could not understand my new way of thinking.

However, there are two things I did learn from my dad that I still live by to this day. He would always say, "Kid, you will probably never have a lot of money, but if you want to go anyplace in this world, always keep your word. If you tell someone you will be there at ten o'clock and you show up at 10:05, you've lied. Remember, your word is your bond."

The other thing he told me was never to go into debt. He reminded me to always pay my way and then some. If I couldn't afford it, he said I shouldn't go into debt to buy it. I built my first health studio in 1936 on that advice, and now that I am in my nineties, I still follow that philosophy to this day. What my dad couldn't give me in a physical way put me in a position to be a success in the fledgling profession of physical fitness and gave me the basic tools to be a successful businessman.

Dick Locher

A Pulitzer Prize–winning political cartoonist, Dick Locher is widely recognized for his astute commentary on American life. His work is nationally syndicated and has appeared in Time, Newsweek, Life, U.S. News & World Report, *and the* Chicago Tribune, *where he has worked since 1973.*

My father repeated these quotes often:

> *"Childhood lasts all through life. It returns to animate broad sections of adult life. Poets will help us find this living childhood within us, this permanent, durable, immobile world."* —GASTON BACHELARD

"The secret to success is sincerity. If you can fake that,
you've got it made." —JEAN GIRAUDOUX

When I was little, Dad's tree loomed above every-thing else in the whole world. He didn't put it up early, it had to wait till Christmas Eve. It was the most magical thing I had ever seen. But then, my dad made my whole life magic.

Nils Lofgren

Nils Lofgren is a singer, a songwriter, a guitarist, and a founding member of Neil Young's band Crazy Horse. A much-sought-after studio musician, he also tours as a solo artist when not on the road with Bruce Springsteen's E Street Band.

My dad always was and still is my hero. Without a doubt, he was the greatest man I've ever known. His honor, integrity, humor, and compassion had a lighthearted, natural depth that was so compelling— he seemed to pull everyone around him up to a higher level. Dad quietly lightened and brightened the mood of every room he was in. Philosophy was one of his life-long hobbies and passions, and he spoke often with a humble awe of what a gift all life is. His great rever-ence for all life was contagious and inspiring. His name is Nils, same as mine.

I'm the oldest of four lucky sons. Our dad fell in love and married our wonderful mother after serving his country as a pilot in World War II. Both were raised as American citizens. Dad's folks were Swedish immigrants and Mom's folks were Italian immigrants, bravely seeking a better life for their kids in America. Even my old-country Sicilian grandfather, after the initial horror of his daughter being courted by my non-Catholic, non-Italian dad, came around to loving him and counting his blessings after realizing what a decent, solid man he was. Together, our folks created a healthy, nurturing environment for us to grow and flourish in. The consequences for our behavior were extremely consistent. We were never ignored or fawned over; the discipline and rewards were guiding and nurturing. Dad inspired so much respect that a small change in the tone of his voice would usually have us doing a quick U-turn back in the right direction. Sure, we all made mistakes, including Dad, but, without ego or fear, he helped us to accept our mistakes as a normal part of life meant to be owned and handled with humility and dignity.

Like many young kids, I was fond of sports. Dad always had time to play them all with us, gently coaching and encouraging. His joy matched ours, and it was contagious. His laughter during touch football games with my brothers in our side yard on Wilmett Court, in

Bethesda, Maryland, remains a vivid memory, so pure and safe, telling us all was right in our world.

My dad showed me how to oil and form my baseball glove, and built a small, portable set of parallel bars to practice gymnastics on. When I was a young, struggling musician, he built me a synthesizer table that I still cherish and use in my garage studio. He taught us to embrace and respect our passions and interests, along with the tools necessary for each one. He never seemed to work at being there for us; he just was. In fact, his spirit still is. I see it every day in my three brothers, who are kind, honorable men and fathers.

Dad permanently stamped my soul with his blend of common sense and compassion. Though many a time, on my own winding road, the rebel in me careened into the dark side, I believe it was Dad's influence and the loving family he and Mom created that compelled me to ask for help and seek the light before mine ever dimmed too far.

Mom and Dad had a passion for dancing together. Because of their love of music and appreciation for its healing qualities, they encouraged me and believed in me on my bumpy road as a young, professional rock-and-roll musician in the mid-1960s—despite the intense disapproval from our Middle America community. I could not have made it without their love and support.

Dad was kind and friendly to all, acquaintances and

strangers alike. He endeared himself with genuine interest and understanding and would usually find some wonder and encouragement for your personal journey. He gave you a respect and space, though never at the expense of his own principles. I'll never forget once at a large family gathering out on the patio at our home, one of our relatives used a racial slur during the course of conversation. My dad, who was ever the kind, gracious host, turned from the grill and with a stern, chilling tone addressed the entire group and bluntly stated, "It is never acceptable to use that kind of language in this home!" Coming from mellow Dad, this was a harsh, startling scolding. As the gravity of the reprimand set in through the uncomfortable silence, he let everyone off the hook by returning to his normal persona and tone with the inquiry, "Now how would you all like your burgers cooked?" The ominous cloud lifted, and the party carried on with a new respect for the ground rules and the man flipping the burgers.

We lost Dad to Alzheimer's in 1997. It was a rough eleven-year good-bye from his diagnosis, just as he was preparing to retire, until his death. Mom and Dad had plans to travel, spend more time with us and their eleven grandkids, and embrace and enjoy retirement. I know they would have. Dad's Alzheimer's diagnosis was a cruel and devastating blow to all of us, especially him and Mom.

I felt so angry and helpless, yet Dad kept loving us

and teaching us even as he navigated that awful road. Early on, when he had to give up driving, one of his favorite skills, I was amazed at how he handled the disappointment. Of course, he had spent his working life in the traffic-safety field and had been instrumental in getting the seat-belt laws passed. His reverence for how critical safe driving is must have had a lot to do with the grace with which he handled it. Always open to helping others and possessing a calm, clear speaking voice, he took a volunteer job reading the newspaper on the radio for those who couldn't read. He embraced the opportunity and took pride and comfort in it until the day he had to give it up due to his own failing abilities. Dad's willingness to openly discuss his pain and his acceptance of each loss remains a great lesson in dignity and courage.

We would go for walks together at Great Falls in Potomac, Maryland, a beautiful forest park with a path along the waterway. After a while, Dad would say, "Feel like jogging a bit, Son?"

"Sure, Dad," I'd reply, and off we'd go. I could see him soaking up the fall air, feeling it blow through his wispy hair and embracing the shaky command he still had of his body, knowing it was being taken from him along with everything else. I thought I was keeping my dad company, but in those precious moments I was again and forever his student, learning from a master how to live every moment, how to find beauty in a tragic journey not of your own choosing. Years later, when he was unable to walk or speak, I would push him in a wheelchair through the same fall breeze, steering with one hand, gently rubbing his shoulder with the other, talking to him and singing his praises, hoping the beautiful fall colors and sounds might bring him a peaceful moment.

I've stepfathered one son into manhood and am currently stepfathering a young teenager along with his mother, Amy, the most beautiful, loving wife I could imagine. Amy grew up without a father. He left her mom and four toddler daughters behind as he wrestled the demons of alcoholism and addiction through eight rehabs (back then they were in primitive mental institutions). He died tragically when Amy was sixteen, she having never known her father or his family.

The only information she ever had about him was negative and bitter. When she was a young mother herself, this incomplete picture of her father manifested itself in a spiritual malady that compelled her to go on a quest for a more complete understanding of who her dad was. She sought and found her father's family and came to learn that he was not all bad. He danced, sang, laughed, and played the piano, and he was tortured by his inability to be the father he wanted to be to the daughters he both loved and devastated. Amy's years of painful, emotional work with Al-Anon and counseling have resulted in love and forgiveness for her dad and a peace and wholeness in her own life as a mother and a woman. I am so proud of her and grateful she is doing the hard work to heal because the powerful, mythical force that is our fathers is inevitable.

I so wish God had given my dad more time here on earth to grace us all with his presence. As a man, a husband, and a stepfather, I am still inspired by Dad's spirit to travel a higher road that rarely is my first choice. It was always his.

As I get older and learn more of friends' painful family journeys, I realize how unusual and rare my "functional" family is. In many a circle, the family/father issues are so messed up and crazy that when I tell my story *I* become the freak. Lucky me, I'll take it!

Looking back, all the big and little things my dad did loom larger and larger. I realize that he didn't just choose to behave like a great dad—he was, by his very nature, a great, loving father.

Dad, I'll never be you; no one could. However, spending my life trying to live by your example brings me a peace and dignity I could never have found without you. Thanks, Dad. I feel your precious presence and your magnificent spirit, and they are beacons that still guide me every day.

All my love, forever.

Your grateful son, Nils.

Susan Lucci

Best known for playing Erica Kane on All My Children, *Susan Lucci has been honored with more acting nominations than any other performer in the history of television. In 1999, she won an Emmy for Outstanding Lead Actress in a Drama Series, and in 2005 she was awarded a star on the Hollywood Walk of Fame.*

I remember so much about my father. He was truly the best father a girl could have. I remember going out to Sunday dinners when I was eight years old. My father would strike up conversations with people at neighboring tables. "This is Susan," he'd say proudly, "the brains of the family." During family dinners at home, he'd throw out brainteasers. Anytime I got the answer, I'd sneak a look at his profile and see how pleased he was—a little crinkle at his eyes and a smile across his face.

He spent time with me, and did so happily, which made me feel incredibly special. He took me horseback riding and ice-skating, and taught me about art—how to draw, paint with watercolors, sketch with charcoal. He even took piano lessons with me to keep me company since I wasn't too happy taking them by myself. That takes a special father.

He was such a good man, with a deep sense of community and empathy. Whenever there was a hurricane or blizzard, which happened quite frequently on Long Island, New York, he was the first one out there, driving around to see if anyone needed help. And I was right there with him in the front seat. I vividly remember the sense of pride that filled me when I'd jump into the car with him.

To be honest, my father wasn't thrilled when I chose acting as a profession—he was worried about me and didn't want me to face a life of rejection. But it was too late. By that time he had given me so much confidence and courage, it never occurred to me that I wouldn't be able to pursue anything I wanted to.

My father set the bar very high for the man who was going to be in my life. He was very much a gentleman, always taking my mother's arm and my arm whenever we crossed the street. I knew that was how a man should be. And I did marry a gentleman like that. My husband treats me that way, he treats my daughter that way, and my son knows how to act like a gentleman by watching his example.

Cardinal Adam Maida

Four years after being named archbishop of Detroit by Pope John Paul II, Adam Maida was named a cardinal and elevated to the College of Cardinals at a consistory at the Paul VI auditorium in the Vatican. Following the pope's death, Cardinal Maida traveled to the Vatican as a cardinal elector to participate in the papal conclave that selected Pope Benedict XVI.

Twenty years after I was ordained a priest, I was driving and listening to the radio in my hometown of Pittsburgh and heard a discussion about people who, for one reason or another, have had a great influence on another person's life. The man calling in said the person who meant the most to him was Adam Maida. That was my father! The caller described how, as a young black man in a factory town, he had struggled in his early years to make ends meet. Adam Maida, he said, trusted him and gave him his start. He would put coal on a borrowed truck, letting him sell it and pay back what he owed when he could. It took some time, the caller said, but eventually he was able to buy his own truck, establish his own delivery business, and pay back everything that had been forwarded to him. "It wouldn't have happened," he said, "without Adam Maida believing in me."

Yes, that was my father—a man of kindness and integrity. He was a man of courage who, as the oldest of eleven children living on a poor farm in Poland, made his way to America as a teenager and settled in the coal country of Pennsylvania. Although he had no formal education, he was able to make enough money to help six of his siblings emigrate to the United States, Canada, and South America.

Growing up with my two brothers, I also remember my father as a man of prayer. He and my mother would get on their knees with us at night as we offered our daily prayers of thanksgiving.

He died in 1971 at the age of sixty-one. I was close to him and miss him terribly. He is remembered every day in my prayers and at Mass.

Don Mattingly

A winner of nine Gold Glove awards, Don Mattingly was the premier first baseman of his era. He won the American League batting championship in 1984 and the league's Most Valuable Player Award in 1985. He is sixth all-time among New York Yankees in career hits.

The biggest thing I think I learned from my father was that he never criticized my play. He criticized my behavior at times in my life, but when it came to baseball, basketball, or football—whatever—he never criticized my play, never put emphasis on it good or bad. He just kind of let me play. He got me to the park and involved in sports but was never really part of "I think you gotta do this, you gotta do that, you didn't hustle, you didn't do this." He just let me play. What this did was give me a joy for playing. I enjoyed playing. I watch Little League dads now, and I see kids that don't play after a certain time. I don't think they enjoy playing. If they don't win, after every game, they know something's coming. With me, I didn't think about it at the time, but later on, it was big because I loved playing. I never had the fear of being really criticized after a game.

Don McLean

An accomplished singer-songwriter, Don McLean is best known for the 1971 hit "American Pie." He was elected to the National Academy of Popular Music Songwriters Hall of Fame in 2004.

Although my father died when I was fifteen years old, he taught me several things that I have tried to teach my kids.

1. Never get into debt.
2. Tell the truth—do not keep secrets.
3. Look up information about things—don't guess.
4. You can always do better.

These are old-fashioned ideas today, but he was old (forty-one) when I came along in 1945, so he passed on concepts he learned during the Depression.

Although he is very distant to me now, I always followed his teaching, and when other "stars" went bankrupt, I always had money, not debts. He never went to college, and after he died, even though I had quit college to become a singer in 1964, I realized my musical career would not happen soon, and I went back to college and graduated in 1968 with a B.B.A. degree. I did this for my father—to make peace with his memory. I then went back into the music business and did well. The college I graduated from (Iona College) gave me an honorary doctorate in 2001. I thought of my father that day.

Joe Morgan

Baseball legend Joe Morgan's many honors include three most valuable player awards. He was elected to the Baseball Hall of Fame in 1990, and now serves as an analyst on ESPN.

M y dad's words:
"Respect policemen; they may be the best friends you ever had."

Ralph Nader

An activist who has worked for decades on environmental, pro-democracy, and consumer-rights issues, advocate, attorney, and author Ralph Nader has also been a presidential candidate as leader of the Green Party in 1996 and 2000.

One of the ways my father taught me was from the remarks he made arising out of normal conversation at our dinner table. Here are two such lessons that I have treasured to this day:

1. "If you don't use your rights, you'll lose your rights."
2. "Almost everyone will claim they love their country. If that is true, why don't they spend more time improving it?"

Kevin Nealon

Actor-comedian Kevin Nealon was the longest-running cast member of Saturday Night Live, *and in 1988 was nominated for an Emmy for his writing work on the show. His films include* The Wedding Singer *and* Roxanne.

Growing up, I helped my father repair and build things around the house. My father, an aeronautical engineer, taught me that if you're going to build or fix something, do it right—make sure the angles are correct and the surfaces are level, and don't downplay the usefulness of glue and clamps. Everything was absolutely level in our house. When my parents went to a swap meet, my mother would naturally be interested in the merchandise for sale in the booth, but my father would be interested in how the booth was constructed. He would analyze the material, the support beams, and the type of rope and knots used to tie it down.

Unfortunately, Dad seldom had the right tools to do the job around our house because my brothers and I would always forget to put them back where they belonged. I watched as he repaired things by improvising tools.

My father taught me that you don't always need the right tools to get the right results. For example:

- The side of a plumber's wrench can be used as a hammer.

- A yard is never too small for the grass to be cut with a sit-down tractor mower.

- Fixing something "for now" means that it is as fixed as it's going to get with tape. There will be no more fixin' until it falls apart again. At that time it can be fixed "for now" again.

- You don't really have to know how to whistle

to get drivers to slow down as they speed past your house. Just put your two fingers in your mouth and blow hard. It will have the intensity of a whistle except for the noise. Follow that immediately by yelling, "Hey, slow down!"

- You should take your time in life, especially when photographing someone when the sun is glaring in their eyes.

- A good nap in the afternoon gives you more energy for another nap later in the day.

- If, during a slide show, a slide is in the projector sideways or upside down, you can correct it by turning the entire projector on its side or upside down.

- There is no limit to the amount of items that can be strapped to the roof of your car, providing you use the correct slipknots.

- There is no food that doesn't taste better cooked in brown sugar.

- Milk is always much more refreshing in a glass full of ice cubes and a large splash of root beer. Also, it's not a bad idea to keep the used glass in the freezer for future use.

- A nice big bowl or two of ice cream at night, right before bed, just "hits the spot."

And, of course, expressions from his generation:

"I have a bum leg" (a nonworking leg).
"The stereo is on the fritz" (it's broken).
"Let me spell you" (relieve you).
"Hold one . . ." (wait a minute).
"Deep-six that!" (get rid of it).

Laraine Newman

A comedian and an actress who began her career with the famed Groundlings troupe in Los Angeles, Laraine Newman was a founding cast member of Saturday Night Live *and appeared on the show from 1975 to 1980.*

My dad was what used to be called a "tough customer" in some respects. Although he was an affectionate, highly intelligent man with a sensational sense of humor, he didn't take shit from anyone.

My dad's first and biggest emphasis was on honesty. He has practical reasons as well as ethical ones. "If you're going to lie, you sure as hell better remember it." What wasn't said, but strongly implied, was "Who wants to live in a world without trust?" He told me my good word was probably one of the most important things I could possess.

The second thing he taught me just by his anecdotes

about growing up Jewish in a small town in Arizona was not to let anyone get away with anti-Semitic remarks or actions. My grandpa was a cowboy who searched out the man who called my dad a "sheeney" and beat him up. Yes, I come from a long line of "tough Jews."

My dad died on January 11, 2004. I was crazy with grief for well over a year. Instead of booting black tar heroin, I mainlined ice cream and cookies and gained forty pounds. About five months ago, I was in a business situation where someone was trying to use my likeness and comments without paying me. My first reaction was to be in a tizzy of fear. Then I asked myself, "What would Arnold do?" I found my father's spirit and toughness was alive and well in me, and I prevailed.

Ted Nugent

Also known as the Motor City Madman, Ted Nugent is a guitarist from Detroit who has sold more than 35 million albums. His hit songs include "Cat Scratch Fever" and "Wango Tango."

Without question, my father taught me the foundation of all quality of life—DISCIPLINE! Warren Henry Nugent was a drill sergeant in the U.S. Army cavalry in World War II, and he ran the Nugent household with a heavy hand. Sometimes a bit too heavy, I suppose, but he sure steered all of us on the straight and narrow, for which I am eternally grateful. His firm hand taught us to not waste, to be thoughtful about our cause and effect, to know and obey the Ten Commandments, and to conduct ourselves courteously and conscientiously.

As a sportsman, he drilled into our heads the positive joys that were a direct result of our safe, attentive firearms training, and that all actions have consequences. I instill this into my own children, and clearly America is in desperate need of more of this "higher level of awareness" discipline today.

Keith Olbermann

Keith Olbermann is the host of Countdown with Keith Olbermann, *a nightly news show on MSNBC. He may be best known for anchoring* ESPN's SportsCenter *from 1992 to 1997, when his inimitable style made the blend of pop culture and sports a hallmark of the modern television sports reporter.*

L ong ago, when I was still at my first job, I was offered a new one with a very new radio network, and another new one at a local station in another city. I much preferred the network job, but I was concerned about the place's long-term viability and that I might be making a mistake. I asked my father about it, and he had a very simple way of analyzing it. "You have this current job, right?" I answered yes. "And they offered you this job you're turning down in Boston, right?" Again I affirmed. "And then there's this job you want to take. Correct?" I agreed. "Then, so what if it is a mistake? Do you really think the only three jobs you'll ever be offered will have come in the first two years of your career?" His point was proved. By my estimation, I've been offered twenty jobs since that day.

Donna Orender

An all-American basketball player at Queens College in New York, Donna Orender played professionally for the Women's Basketball League, where she was an all-star. She currently serves as commissioner of the WNBA.

My dad, Gerald Leon Chait, looms large in my life. He's all about working hard and achieving. He's the kind of dad who looked at a report card full of A's and asked, "Why the one B?" He always challenged me to be better and instilled a work ethic, and that ethic is like a little internal buzz saw that always keeps humming.

He inspired in me my love of sports. It was an easy conversation to have with him. "How'd the Mets do today, Dad?" From there I got a report on Ed Kranepool and Art Shamsky, maybe Cleon Jones and Tom Seaver.

Despite my dad's concerns as I got older about my playing sports—it wasn't what girls did back then—he knew I loved basketball. There was no such thing as the portable hoops we have today. He had to dig the hole, set the cement, and sink the eleven-foot pole. He nearly broke his back setting that pole, but he did it for me, and I was always grateful. I still am, as basketball became my ticket to the world.

Dottie Pepper

A seventeen-time tournament winner on the LPGA Tour, including two major championships, Dottie Pepper made six appearances for the United States in the Solheim Cup and today works as a commentator for NBC and the Golf Channel.

My dad, Don Pepper, was an AAA all-star baseball player in 1968 and was on the cover of *Sports Illustrated* that year. He taught me as a youngster to always look professional when I went to the golf course; he felt it was a huge part of the "job." I was not allowed to go to practice or play without my shoes being polished, clothes neat, and clubs clean. He followed the same practices when he played both minor- and major-league baseball; he was even caught polishing his spikes in the dugout. I can honestly say that I have never played a round with dirty shoes or wrinkled clothes.

He continues to this day polishing his shoes before going to work each day . . . all a part of looking professional.

Tony Perez

A major-league baseball player who was a key member of Cincinnati's "Big Red Machine" in the 1970s, Tony Perez also played for the Montreal Expos, the Boston Red Sox, and the Philadelphia Phillies. In 2000, he was elected to the Baseball Hall of Fame.

When I was seventeen years old, I left my home in Cuba to play baseball in the United States, not knowing when I would see my father and the rest of my family again. Before I left, he said to me, "Son, much success, but never forget the lessons learned in our nest."

Joe Perry

As the lead guitarist and a contributing songwriter for the long-standing, multiplatinum rock-and-roll band Aerosmith, Joe Perry helped earn the group four Grammy Awards and an induction into the Rock and Roll Hall of Fame. In 2005, his eagerly awaited solo album was released.

M y dad was the strong and silent type. The life lessons I learned from him were by his example, and the two strongest ones were these: the importance of balancing family and work, and with hard work and perseverance you can accomplish anything.

It seemed no matter how busy he was with work, he still found time to drive two and a half hours to meet us every weekend during our summer vacations in New Hampshire, or just to check in and work on little projects together. Everything mattered, no matter how big or small. Work is important, but family is everything. I couldn't think of living life any other way.

His parents were Portuguese immigrants who worked hard to make ends meet in their new country. Dad went on to get a college degree and, with my mother, built a better life for my sister and me. I saw him giving 110 percent to whatever he did, whether it be his career, constructing our summer cabin in New Hampshire, or upholding the position of town treasurer.

My only regret is that he isn't here today to see how happy I am with the beautiful family I have. He passed away when I was twenty-three. I was, however, able to share with him my first gold album when he was sick in the hospital.

So, Dad, the hard work paid off in ways neither of us could have imagined. I know the impact of your example on me is the reason why I am as successful as I am today. Thanks so much, Dad. I miss you and love you.

Robert Pinsky

Robert Pinsky is a frequently honored essayist, educator, and translator. His work The Figured Wheel: New and Collected Poems, 1966–1996 *was nominated for the Pulitzer Prize. He served as poet laureate of the United States from 1997 to 2000.*

My father, Milford Simon Pinsky, was a gifted athlete. His advice to me playing sports was not easy to follow: "Take it easy." He had many practical, cautious, tough sayings, similar to what the Fool tries to tell King Lear.

My daughter Nicole once did up some of Milford Pinsky's wisdom in calligraphy for me, and gave the list to me framed:

Take It Easy.

Never Catch Behind the Plate Without a Mask.

Let the Other Guy Play the Tip on a Horse,
   You Take the Cash.

Avoid Fights.

If You Can't Avoid a Fight, Get in the First Punch.

The Average Winning Hand in Seven-Card Stud
   Is a High Two Pair.

Respect Knives.

Don't Try to Kill the Ball.

Use Your Head.

Before You Marry a Girl, Look at Her Mother.

Be Polite.

What I get from these is less the specific advice than an outlook: generous, prudent, sensible.

John "Bucky" Pizzarelli

For more than half a century, John "Bucky" Pizzarelli has been a part of the fraternity of musicians who have kept mainstream and traditional jazz alive. The list of big bands and vocalists with whom Bucky has performed and recorded reads like a veritable who's who of jazz. The father of John Pizzarelli Jr., he has been a fixture in jazz and the studios since the early 1950s.

We had a grocery store during the Depression. I guess I was five when my dad bought the store. All the banks were closed up and he struggled through that thing. What he did was he trusted a lot of people who didn't have any money. There was no cash around in those days. We never knew the difference. We went through the whole Depression and never knew there was a Depression. Basically, we saw everybody had the same hardships, and they were doing without cash. The teachers got paid in scrip. They would come to the store and get whatever they needed. My father would have to go down and cash in the scrip at city hall for his money. Everything hinged around trust. He took everybody straight through the Depression. He carried the whole neighborhood. Everybody was on the books.

Little by little, eventually, by the time World War II ended in 1945, he had a big list of debts that were never paid. But it didn't faze him at all. We got everything we needed and we all ate well because we had the store and we had regard for other people and it would carry through. When I went with Vaughn Monroe's band after the war, my dad would always get the truck—it didn't matter how late he worked in the store—and meet us on the highway as we were coming back from a one-nighter and take all the guys who lived in Jersey and drive them home. Everybody had a ride home at four in the morning. That's the way he was. He was also a boxer, and we went to a lot of boxing matches and wrestling matches. He told me what to do whenever you encountered a bully. Actually, a bully in the neighborhood would always bully somebody in front of other people. He said the best way to get those guys would be to get them alone and give them one good shot and knock them down all by yourself with nobody watching and they would never bother you again.

John Pizzarelli

Since age six, John Pizzarelli has been playing guitar, following in the tradition of his father, jazz guitar legend Bucky Pizzarelli. Hailed by critics as one of the most accomplished interpreters of the Great American Songbook, he is known for his brilliant guitar work and smooth vocals. In a career that has produced eighteen recordings and gained international recognition, he has brought classic standards to a new generation.

The first things I think about are lessons in music, but actually they end up applying to everything else. There are two answers that I've always thought of. One of them is about efficiency. Starting in the 1960s, my father always taught us to get to the airport early. It's haunted all of my friends who have gone to the airport with me. My father has always had us at the airport at least three hours early just to hang out. He'd say, "You always gotta be at the gate no matter what," and we always were. If anything got screwed up, my father would turn to us and say, "I told you, you gotta get to the airport an hour earlier than when we got here." Even if an hour earlier was the day before.

The other thing that stuck with me, too, which is most important, I think, and that I realized as I worked with him was that every gig counts. There was always that sense no matter where we were going to play together—and we played everywhere and anywhere we could between 1980 and 1990. We played in senior citizens' homes, we played in clubs where they talked through us playing together, we played at private parties where we sat on stairways. But he never said to me, "Ah, we're just gonna play a party, nobody's gonna listen, don't worry about it." He was always in the game. He was always ready to go to play. So what would happen would be that at all of those little four-hour gigs where maybe nobody listened, even though you could tell there were some people listening, you knew you were always going to change somebody's life along the way.

We had twenty-five minutes of material because we

played four hours at these parties where we were really working on stuff. We could do half an hour without thinking. We would leave and say, "That was twenty-five of the easiest minutes," because all of the four-hour gigs counted. We never treated any of those gigs like they didn't matter. We were always prepared. That was the thing. Every gig counted, and that was big.

The other thing I was told was that it was just as good to be part of a large ensemble as it was to be the star soloist in front of that ensemble. My dad always said, "I'd love to play rhythm guitar in that group" or "I'd love to be in that band," as opposed to "I'd love to be the soloist with that band." He loved the fact that it was just as much fun for him to play in a band with seventeen other guys than it was for him to be the one guy who got up in front and played. It was about the ensemble, not just about being a great soloist yourself, but also about being someone who can add something to a group just by your smallest amount of participation.

Susan Polgar

A four-time World Chess champion and a five-time Olympic champion, Susan Polgar is internationally recognized as the first woman to break the gender barrier in chess.

I vividly remember all the good times I had with my father. One day at around the age of four, I accidentally discovered a chess set. Being so curious about the funny shapes of the chess pieces, my four-year-old inquiring mind wanted to know what they were. I asked my mother. "They are chess pieces," she said. "Wait until your father gets home and he will show you." That was how history was made.

My father was very happy that I was curious to know. He started to show me what they were. He had the knack to make it all sound like fairy tales with a "king and queen living in a beautiful castle." He made up funny and interesting games such as Pawn Wars. Even though my father was not such an expert in the game, his way of sharing the beauty of chess made an incredible impact on me for the rest of my life.

For years after that day, he taught me chess and, of course, guided me in many other aspects of life. Besides chess, he also taught me math and got me involved in sports.

He taught me in principle what is right and wrong in life. He always stressed the importance of being a good sport and being modest. He has an incredibly strong work ethic. He always said, "Hard work will have its fruits!" In other words, diligence will pay off. He is certainly right there, and those were the words I have always followed.

He believes that praising children for their accomplishments is extremely important. Therefore, it is important to give them tasks that they can succeed at so they can accomplish them and earn praise: "Good job! Well done! Wow, you are so smart. You are brilliant!" It certainly motivated me to achieve and succeed more and more.

He is also a man with vision. He set goals that many people had a hard time imagining and believing were doable. But he believes that unless you set a high standard, you will never fulfill your abilities.

Because of the strong values in my upbringing, I was able to accomplish the impossible throughout my life. When most people believed that women could never play chess as well as men do, I set my goals for the ultimate. I proved time and time again that women can succeed in the men's world if they work hard at it. In my thirty-year career, I broke countless gender, religious, and age barriers in chess.

In 1986, I became the first woman to qualify for the Men's World Chess Championship cycle. Even though I was *not* allowed to compete that year because I was a woman, the rules were changed and the word "Men's" was removed.

In January 1991, I became the first woman to earn the men's Grandmaster title. My baby sister, Judit, followed in my footsteps and became the second woman in history to do the same later that year, in December.

In 1996, I became the first World Chess Champion in history (male or female) to win the Triple Crown in

Chess (Blitz, Rapid, and Classical world chess championships). In 2004, I played competitive chess again after nearly nine years of retirement to lead the 2004 U.S. Women's Olympic Team to the first-ever team medal. We ended up with a historic team silver, and I also captured another three individual medals (two gold and one silver), bringing my total medal count to five gold, four silver, and one bronze. I also extended my Olympiad scoring streak to fifty-six consecutive games without a loss.

On August 1, 2005, at the age of thirty-six, I broke four overall world records by playing 326 opponents simultaneously, winning 309 while drawing 14 for a winning percentage of 96.93. I also played 1,131 consecutive games against 551 opponents, winning 1,112 while drawing 16 for an unprecedented winning percentage of 99.02. It took 14,361 steps, more than 9.1 miles, and 16.5 straight hours to accomplish.

I broke many other barriers in my career but probably none of it would have been possible if it was not for my father's influence, support, and guidance. Even at times when I had self-doubt after painful defeats, he always stayed positive and pushed me to try again. He always believed that I would succeed no matter how hard the tasks or how high the goals.

Today, I am a role model for millions of children across the globe. Of course, I would not be where I am without the incredible influence of my mother as well, but that is for another book. Even though I am now living thousands of miles away from my father, his words and influence in me remain strong. Today, I try to instill the same values in my two sons as well as countless other children that I come across on a daily basis. That is my father. He did things his way, and he did things out of love for his daughters.

Jorge Ramos

An Emmy Award–winning anchor for Univision Network News, Jorge Ramos is the author of seven books, including No Borders, The Latino Wave, *and* Dying to Cross. *He writes a weekly column for more than forty newspapers in the United States and Latin America. The oldest of five siblings, he was born in Mexico City in 1958.*

I made peace with my father a few years before he died. And that is one of the best things that I have ever done in my life. No resentments. No unexpressed feelings. No emotional baggage to carry for the rest of my life.

On the contrary, as the Chilean writer Isabel Allende once wisely advised me, the people that we really, really love never die. We carry them in our gestures, in our movements, in our routines. And I carry my father, with lots of love, when I sneeze the same way he did, when I try to trap a mosquito with my hand, or when I talk to my teenage daughter about sex, just like he did with me, while driving to the mall and listening to music.

My father was a strict man. I don't remember ever playing with him, except for one day when he tried to hit a soccer ball and missed miserably. I cried alone in a corner after that incident. When you are young and everything revolves around soccer, you simply cannot forgive your father if his foot misses a melon-size ball. It was then, before I turned ten, that the image of my father as a perfect man broke into tiny pieces.

Later, things got worse. As the firstborn, I grew increasingly apart from Pa, as I used to call him. I had only two choices: to obey him or to defy him. I chose the second one. My youthful rebelliousness created, eventually, a physical distance from him, and when I had the first chance I left Mexico City for Los Angeles. It was January 2, 1983. I was finally liberated. Or so I thought.

Ironically, it was the distance that brought us back together. Once he understood that I was out of his reach, he relaxed, and so did I. No more challenging conversations. No more abrupt responses. No more turning our backs in the middle of a shouting match.

At a distance, my father suddenly became a very warm and vulnerable man. His physique had been severely affected because of a brain hemorrhage and two heart attacks. But, somehow, the decline of his body brought out the wonderful human being he had been hiding all his life.

Meanwhile, I became anchorman for Univision Network News in Miami and, thanks to the expanding satellite technology, he watched me every single night from his home in Mexico City. Knowing this, I used to call him immediately after the evening newscast to get his opinion on the news of the day. But more often than not, he would say, "I don't know about that, I simply tuned in to watch you." To hear that made me smile with contentment. It seemed he had also made peace with me. What a wonderful change! Finally I could get to know my real father. It was not always like that.

I remember that right before college, when I announced to him that I wanted to study communication, he blurted, "But what are you going to do with that?" "I don't have the slightest idea," I responded in defiance, "but I just want to study something interesting." And that's what I did. However, I always knew that he would have been happier had I chosen a different profession, like architecture, engineering, medicine, or law.

As the years went by, I made a mental note to myself not to follow in my father's footsteps. We had the same name, Jorge Gilberto. That was enough. He had become an architect and definitely had a talent for it. But it seemed to me that he never truly enjoyed his work. What he really liked was magic. Yes, my father, in his heart, always wanted to be a magician.

Whenever he had the chance, he would perform tricks for our family and friends. It was wonderful to see his face when he came home with a new trick or gimmick from the magic store. I always loved the magician in my father. Suddenly, with the twist of a magic wand in his hand, the serious, impenetrable, complex architect would become a happy, energetic, transparent, and charming magician. He was then, and only then, full of surprises and full of life.

For a few minutes, my father would transform himself into someone different. And I was so proud to have a dad like that. Late, too late in my life, I learned that the magician—not the structured and moody architect—was the true self of my father. And nothing pained me more than to see him going back to his old guarded self after a session of pure magic. But, unbeknownst to him, he was teaching me two powerful lessons.

One, that it is never too late to say I love you and to show your true emotions to those who care about you. And two, that despite all the opposition we may encounter, we have to follow our dreams and do what we enjoy the most. Life is too short and messy to do otherwise. My father didn't follow his true calling—to be a magician—and he paid dearly for it. But I learned from his mistakes. And thanks to him I have a better, more complete life.

Every once in a while I get a jolt of surprise when I discover in me another move, another gesture, that used to define my father. The latest discovery is that we both yawn in the same rude and noisy way. And when that happens, I realize that in many ways my father, the magician, lives deep in me.

Sally Jessy Raphael

After hosting a radio call-in advice show for six years, Sally Jessy Raphael became a household name as a result of having her own television talk show, Sally, *which ran in first-run syndication from 1985 to 2002. Today, she hosts the Internet radio show* Sally JR's Open House.

"Sally, I don't ever want you to learn how to type."

"I never even thought of learning how to do that," I replied.

My dad reminded me that in his day, a person who learned to type did not become an executive in top management. He wanted the best for me. He always said I could be anything I wanted to be.

Della Reese

A multitalented film and television actress, Della Reese is perhaps best known for her role as Tess on the inspirational television drama Touched by an Angel. *In 1987, she was nominated for a Grammy Award as best female soloist in gospel music.*

My father, Richard Thad Early, was my hero. He literally poured steel for Detroit Steel Products for thirty-seven years. When he retired, they put in a machine because the work my father had been doing all those years then became considered unsafe for humans.

He was my hero because he was always there for me and I always felt his great love for me. I appreciated that he always knew what to do, sometimes immediately, but always, eventually, he would work it out.

When I was leaving Detroit for New York to start my career, I of course went to my father for worldly advice. I was prepared for some philosophical words when I asked him what I should do, but instead he said to me, "You can do whatever you want to if you only find the"—and then he made the clicking noise you make when you suck the inside of your cheek toward your teeth—"in it."

Since then, the successes I have had were due to finding that certain little "click" in them before I started out. You can do anything if you can find the niche in it, the catch in it, the central operative cord or string, or the trick of it; or the sound of the "click" of your jaw in it. It calls for investigation and understanding.

Kurt Russell

Kurt Russell is an actor known for films such as Escape from New York, 3000 Miles to Graceland, Backdraft, *and* Silkwood. *During his prolific and successful career, he has appeared in more than fifty feature films and been nominated for many awards, including an Emmy and a Golden Globe.*

I guess I'm living my life a lot like my dad. My dad, Bing, was a professional baseball player—and I played pro ball. My dad was an actor—and I act. I think my dad had a good life, and I think I'm continuing to follow in his footsteps.

My dad died in April 2003, but he was really fun. He had big laughs. Acting took us to different places together. When I was a teenager, shooting a Disney film called *Guns in the Heather,* he and I lived, for a few months, in Dromoland Castle in Ireland. While we were there, we played golf all over Ireland.

My dad was a really good player—not too many years before he died, he won the Maine state amateur championship—but he really knew games and how to gamble. In a bar, before a golf match, he had this amazing ability to size up the guy next to him by listening to him talk. He could virtually see right through him and within half an hour, he knew how many strokes the guy was lying by. Most of the time, he found a guy who thought he was a little bit better than he was, and it was fun for my dad to win money off of that person. He loved doing that, he really did. He liked pushing himself.

Even when I was a teenager, my dad and I played guys for money. We won a couple thousand dollars a number of times. I remember we played a highly ranked professional who made a very bad mistake—he got drunk with my dad in a bar the night before. By the time we got to the fifteenth hole, he was down more than $4,000. The guy said, "This is a buzz saw. I want out . . . now." My dad let him pay what he owed us to that point and leave.

So on the rare occasions when my dad had losing moments on the golf course, it wasn't because of his mouth or brain.

Bob Saget

Bob Saget is an actor and a comedian whose television work includes Full House, *which he starred in from 1987 to 1995, and* America's Funniest Home Videos, *which he hosted from 1990 to 1997. He is also noted for his stand-up comedy routines and his cameo roles in feature films.*

About fifteen years ago, my uncle Bill was in the intensive care heart ward at Cedar Sinai Hospital in Los Angeles. My dad, Ben, and I went to go see him. My father and mother have been through more than most parents. They've lost four children, and my father lost all four of his younger brothers. I tell you this to set up a simple story.

We got on an elevator in the hospital with a woman we didn't know. She was crying. It was just the three of us. My father looked at this woman, a stranger, and after a beat of silence said, "Has anyone told you that you look beautiful today?"

It was not the words, but his face—the warmness with which he had just complimented her. You would have thought an angel had spoken to her. Her face lit up, then she looked into his eyes and said, "Thank you." He didn't say anything else. For a brief instant, he had taken her out of her grief. When the doors opened, she smiled and got off the elevator.

So I'd say the most important life lesson my father has imparted to me is perhaps ingrained in that one tiny act of human kindness. Of seeing someone hurting, truly caring, and just letting them know that. He is now eighty-eight and performs acts like this throughout his day. I treasure every moment with him. I just wish he'd stop talking to strangers.

Maria Elena Salinas

Maria Elena Salinas is a coanchor of Noticiero Univision, *the most popular newscast among American Hispanics. Her impressive career has made her the most famous female American Hispanic journalist in the United States.*

I learned more from my father—and about my father—after he passed away. He was a man of contrasts. He was kind, yet distant. He was an intellectual, more interested in instilling moral values in his three daughters than encouraging academic excellence. He was a strong disciplinarian who relied on my mother to enforce his rules. He was a pacifist who avoided confrontation.

My father held strong family values but was estranged from most of his own family in Mexico. He spoke six languages and held a doctorate degree in philosophy, yet he was never successful in business. He worked as a Realtor, an accountant, a bowling alley manager, a professor. But it wasn't big bucks or salary bonuses he seemed to be after. Instead, he was driven by a sense of mission and charity.

As long as I can remember, he had been an enigma. Then, shortly after he died in 1985, I discovered something about him that was both shocking and revealing.

It was a hot summer day in Los Angeles as I tried to get back into the routine of covering the news of the day for KMEX (Channel 34). I was still mourning the loss of my father when the "box of secrets" arrived. At first sight, it seemed to be an ordinary box. An old friend of my father's told me my father had asked him to keep the box in a safe place, well protected from the elements, and from his family.

The box he handed me was full of books, letters, and loose papers, nothing of particular interest. But beneath them was a small, accordion-type file jammed with personal documents, scraps of our lives: birth and baptismal certificates, report cards, family photographs, official letters, paycheck stubs, rent receipts.

Hidden in the compartments were passages of stories he had never told us, letters and documents filled with references to military service, World War II, and alien registration cards. I read through them, learning about a man I had lived with all my life, realizing I knew very little about him.

But the real shock came when I picked up a small booklet celebrating the twenty-fifth anniversary of my uncle Jose Antonio's priesthood. In the acknowledgments, there was a line that read, "I would like to thank those who influenced my sacerdotal vocation, particularly my brother, Father Jose Luis Cordero Salinas." The words hit me like a ton of bricks. In tears, my mother confirmed my findings. Yes, my father had been a Catholic priest. A grave disappointment drew him away from the church before he met her. She assured me that this was all she knew.

Needless to say, the news filled me with all sorts of mixed emotions. There were so many questions, so many doubts, so much more I needed to know. Why did he leave the church? Did my mother have anything to do with it? Why didn't he tell us? I felt that knowing more about my father's past, and understanding what motivated him to be the complex individual he was, would certainly help me understand my own life better. So strong was my need to know that I spent years investigating his past, searching for his estranged family in Mexico, and looking for clues that would help unravel the mysteries of his life. My search inspired a book of my own.

As a child, I appreciated my father's kindness. As a teenager, I feared his firmness. As an adult, I respected and admired his intellect. But it wasn't until after he died that I realized just how much I learned from him and how much I inherited from him. I always wanted to be my mother, but I ended up being my father.

My father taught me the importance of moral values, decency, self-respect, discipline, and formality. He taught me to be proud of my Mexican heritage, even though I am a U.S.-born American citizen. He showed me through example the value of being multilingual.

He taught me that richness of the soul is more valuable than a hefty bank account.

I now believe I inherited from him not only his stubbornness and perfectionism, but also a sense of mission that has driven my life, and a social conscience that has been the backbone of my journalistic career. But there is certainly one thing about my father I will not emulate. I want to be an open book to my own daughters. Unlike him, I want to live a life without secrets.

Ryan Seacrest

Producer and television personality Ryan Seacrest is best known for his work on the hit talent-search show American Idol. *He has also worked for MTV and ESPN, and in 2005 he was awarded a star on the Hollywood Walk of Fame for his impressive contributions to entertainment broadcasting.*

My father is my best friend. He is an attorney in Atlanta, and I always admired his work ethic and passion for both his family and his career. I can remember daydreaming in elementary school when I was young, wondering what it was I was going to do when I grew up. At the time, I was lucky to have a few dollars in the piggy bank from the tooth fairy. Family dinners were sacred at my house as a kid. It was a traditional sit-down meal—the one where Mom made you "finish your plate" and take your dishes to the sink. One night during our evening summit, I asked my dad how he knew what he wanted to do for a living. How can one be sure? At what age did you decide? How do people make a decision like this? The impetus to the question was more typical overanalyzing and obsessing on how I, too, would be able to afford light-bulbs, a table, chairs, and food for my "family dinner" someday. My father gave me some of the best advice I've ever received that night. I was twelve years old, and he told me to identify a passion and make that my career path. It sounded too easy, but he reinforced it by using a quote from Confucius: "Choose a job you love and you'll never have to work a day in your life."

That night I went up to my room after dinner and did what I usually did—pretended to have my own radio show. I had an old pair of Pioneer headphones, the kind that were the same size as those pilots wore. I had a stereo mixer from RadioShack, a Fischer micro-phone, and a cassette tape. On my "show," I would pre-tend to count down the forty biggest songs in the United States. I actually channeled Casey Kasem. I would make these tapes and then give them to my par-ents as Mother's Day or Father's Day gifts, so they could pop them in the cassette player in the car and pretend to be entertained. I had more fun making those tapes than anything else twelve-year-old boys do.

I had more fun than riding a bike, playing basketball, camping, or sneaking a peak at HBO after 9 p.m. on a Saturday. That night I went to bed and realized what my dad was telling me. Find something you love, make it your career, and you will be just fine. At twelve years old, I identified my passion—broadcasting. I knew I wanted to broadcast on radio and maybe someday TV. Tom Connellan said, "One person with passion is better than fifty who are merely interested." From that day on I knew what I wanted. Almost twenty years later, Casey Kasem passed the baton to me. Each week I count down the hits, I thank God for family dinners.

Isadore "Issy" Sharp

A Canadian businessman, Isadore "Issy" Sharp is the chairman and chief executive officer of Four Seasons Hotels and Resorts, a company he founded in 1960. In 1992, he was made an Officer of the Order of Canada.

I believe that principles and values unknowingly inherited last a lifetime and are the most important lessons learned. After I was educated to be an architect, I began my career in the construction business with my father, Max. He was born in 1902 in a small town in Poland called Oświęcim, now better known as Auschwitz. His brother Nathan traced the family tree back more than two hundred years to 1784 and revealed that my father's great-grandfather was a scholar—a chief judge who wrote a book called *Paths of Propriety.* Propriety, integrity, and respect became a family value system handed down for 220 years.

My father's family of seven boys and four girls was forced to separate because of World War I. After the war, he left home and got a visa in Vienna to enter Palestine, where, at the age of eighteen, he helped establish the first kibbutz. After he moved to Canada, he worked as a plasterer for $15 a week. He wanted a raise, but they said no, so he decided to work for himself.

On his first job, he lost everything he had plus his next few years' earnings. Through the Depression, he was in the amusement business selling slot machines and pinball machines, after which he started as a builder. I remember when my father injured his shoulder while excavating a cellar using a horse and plow— but kept on working.

My sisters—Edie, Bea, and Neddy—and I had the precious privilege of a wonderful childhood. We had a home in which our friends were always welcomed, a home in which we learned by example the values and ethics of life. And as we matured, we understood and appreciated more and more the true value of the principles we inherited from our parents.

My father was forever the optimist—and a mild-mannered gentleman. And everyone spoke well of him.

Siegfried & Roy

Master magicians and illusionists, Siegfried & Roy have hosted the most popular performances in Las Vegas for more than thirty years. Siegfried Fischbacher is a traditional magician and illusionist, while Roy Uwe Ludwig Horn is known for his special rapport with exotic animals.

The most important lesson we learned from our fathers is that, like all of us, they were human beings, with all the goodness and the flaws that come with that. Knowing this made them an even bigger source of inspiration for us to go out and follow our dreams.

Steven Slon

Steve Slon is editor in chief of AARP The Magazine. In 2005, he received recognition from the National Magazine Award for the Magazine Section, a category that honors excellence in editorial work. His father, Sidney Slon, died in 1994.

Theater was my father's religion, and Shakespeare's works were his bible. When it came time to teach us a lesson, out would come *Hamlet* or *Othello* or *King Lear*. Using these plays as a moral compass, Dad set me up with some quite precise ideas about how a man should behave in the world.

My father had studied at the Goodman Theatre in Chicago. He was an impossibly good-looking young man—extraordinarily good-looking, come to think of it, in early photographs a lot like Clark Gable, tall and athletic. He was a good actor, too, and proud of his skill. Other dads might sing in the shower, but my dad would recite: "What is he to Hecuba or her to him that he should weep for her?" This he would say in almost English-accented diction, his stage voice, broadcasting the words loudly through the corridors of our apartment on Manhattan's Upper West Side. Other times, he'd perform at the breakfast table or just walking around in his pajamas. After certain passages, there'd be a little gasp, a catch in his throat. Yes, he frequently moved himself to tears. And we, my brother, my sister, and I, were always transfixed. Dad could be bigger than life.

He'd been successful in the thirties, way before I was born. He came to New York from Chicago in the midst of the Depression, nearly penniless but for a tiny allowance from his mother. Within months, he was an announcer on *The Prince Albert Show,* and soon had parts in daytime serials like *Mert and Marge, Valiant Lady,* and *The Goldbergs.* He was sometimes doing two or three live performances in a day, zipping across town in taxis. If you believed him, and you couldn't always, he would also use the trick of hiring an ambulance to cut through the swirl of New York traffic in order to make it to the next reading. Reading, of course, being the operative word, since radio actors often ʼperformed cold, without having rehearsed or even seen the piece beforehand.

His dream had been to perform on the stage, and he would brim with emotion as he told us about great actors he'd seen perform, such as the Lunts and the young Olivier. He never compared his own radio work to stage acting—he felt his work in broadcasting had been just something to pay the bills. Unfortunately, performing on stage in New York was not to be, since this devastatingly handsome man had wrecked his good looks at about age nineteen when, showing off for a girlfriend, he dove into the shallow waters of Lake Michigan and slammed into a rock hidden just below the surface. His nose was shredded, and, plastic surgery being what it was back then, it was never quite right. Picture Clark Gable with Karl Malden's knob in front. I never heard him complain about his looks, or what the accident had cost him, but as far as I know, he never auditioned for the stage after his early twenties. And when television began to overtake radio, he knew better than to stick around. By his midforties, when I was still little, he was out of the business. But he continued always to define himself by the rules of the theater and by the code and ethics of the actor.

I determined at a young age that I, too, would become an actor. My first big performance was in a school play. This was fifth grade, and we had spent the whole semester studying the ancient Greeks. We had read *The Illiad* and *The Odyssey* and now we were performing an adaptation of Aristophanes' *Peace,* in which a farmer travels to heaven astride a giant dung beetle to discuss the follies of war with Zeus. I landed the part of the leader of the chorus. In rehearsal one day, I slipped and fell while prancing about the stage and got a big laugh. Fine. I built up this pratfall, making it bigger and bigger with each succeeding rehearsal.

We performed *Peace* for the entire school. Parents were invited. I mugged my way through my scenes and, of course, for my big finale, I upended myself spectacularly, landing square on my butt. As expected, this completely broke up the audience. The sound of the laughter was thrilling.

Mom came backstage to congratulate me, but Dad for some reason had left. It wasn't until I got home that I had any inkling there was a problem. Still aglow from my smashing success, I rushed into the living room, where he was seated in a chair, wearing his reading glasses, holding a large volume in his lap. He didn't look up when I came in. There were no effusive congratulations, no welcome to the new actor in the family, no hug. A frown creased his forehead.

"Sit down," he said severely, beckoning me to a

chair he had pulled up beside him. My performance had been an embarrassment, he said. Seems I had violated just about every code of conduct in the actor's book, from scene-stealing to shamelessly overacting.

After a lecture about the ethics and responsibilities of the performer, he opened up the book. *Hamlet,* of course. Dad turned to Hamlet's advice to the Players, which, he explained, was Shakespeare's lesson on the actor's craft. If I was ever to be an actor, everything I needed to know was right here.

He began reading: "Speak the speech, I pray you, as I pronounced it to you, trippingly on the tongue: but if you mouth it, as many of our players do, I had as lief the town-crier spoke my lines. Nor do not saw the air too much with your hand, thus, but use all gently: for in the very torrent, tempest, and, as I may say, whirlwind of your passion, you must acquire and beget a temperance that may give it smoothness. O, it offends me to the soul to hear a robustious periwig-pated fellow tear a passion to tatters . . . I could have such a fellow whipped . . ."

After he finished, he had me read it aloud. Then we read it together. We stayed until I could recite it from memory. Finally, he let me go.

The lesson he taught me is not just for the stage. The lesson is for life: Be funny, but don't be a clown; be smart, but don't be a smart aleck.

Don't be such a damn show-off.

Linda Solomon

An award-winning photojournalist, Linda Solomon photographs the Academy Awards each year and has appeared on The Oprah Winfrey Show. *Her photographs can be seen in the book* People We Know—Horses They Love, *which she coauthored with her sister, Jill Rappaport, who is an entertainment reporter for NBC's* Today Show.

Sometimes it is difficult for children to express verbally what is within them. It is safe and fun to express feelings through a camera. I know this personally because my father, Daniel J. Rappaport, gave me a camera when I was five. I was never alone again. With my camera around my neck, my friend was always with me. I have learned the difference between merely looking at and truly seeing life, appreciating the precious moment. His gift of a camera proved a catalyst.

Yet another present will remain in my heart forever. I remember opening a beautifully wrapped box to find a blue leather book with the following words engraved in gold: *Happy 13th birthday. I love you, Dad.* It was a very elaborate and elegant photo album. The album represented encouragement and respect for a child's photographs. Photographs reveal the heart. When I work with children, my photo assignment for them is to capture "what they wish for in life." It sounds so sweet, yet the wishes revealed are very serious. I did not know how to respond when a nine-year-old girl walked up to me and said, "I can't photograph this wish. I wish to have a mom of my own." I found out later that her young mother had recently passed away from AIDS.

Now I always ask children to make a written list of their wishes first. "I wish to help my mom and dad pay the rent" was expressed by an eleven-year-old from Washington, D.C. "I wish to see my mom happy again" were words shared by a ten-year-old boy from Detroit. "I wish for sex offenders to be banned from all parks" was written in a child's hand.

What can we learn from the children's photographs? I discovered that their wishes are for everyone else and so unselfish. I work with children all over the country, yet their wishes are the same in thought, in heart, and in spelling: "I wish for no pollution." "I wish for world peace." "I wish to go to kollege." "I wish everyone believed in God." When you show children that you care about their hopes, their dreams, and their wishes, perhaps you will make a child who has never felt he or she had worth feel special.

The beautiful gift of an album from my father when I was a child is represented now in the wishes and hopes expressed from the hearts of children.

Aaron Spelling

American television and film producer Aaron Spelling has had one of the most prolific and successful careers in show business. He has worked on more than two hundred productions, among them Charlie's Angels, Dynasty, *and* Charmed, *and has founded two successful production companies, Aaron Spelling Productions and Spelling Entertainment.*

I was very happy to be the baby of the family. My mother took care of the older kids and my father took care of me. He took care of me in a special way, and some of the things he did turned my whole life around. He is no longer with us, but some of the things he did for me will stay in my life forever.

For example, he decided that my paper route was too dangerous, so he began to accompany me every morning. In addition, he never missed going with me to collect my monthly payments.

Believe me, some of the collections were not easy. However, without my father, they would have been impossible.

One day, after we had finished my collections, my father told me he was taking me to one of the theaters downtown where a great comic from Hollywood was performing. Although I had all of the money from my paper route, he insisted on paying for the theater tickets. On the way to the theater, he told me that he had waited years to see Eddie Cantor perform. Mr. Cantor was magnificent, but suddenly something happened that was going to affect my life.

During his act, Mr. Cantor slipped on a wet sponge onstage, and he ripped the coat of his handsome suit. He told the audience that he would have to go to his dressing room to change clothes, but he would return soon. My father grabbed my arm and said, "Hallelujah." Then we followed Mr. Cantor to his dressing room. Once there, my father explained that it would be impossible for him to repair the suit there. However, he told Mr. Cantor about his little tailor shop in our backyard. My father told him that if he would accompany him, he would make a suit for Mr. Cantor at no charge. Mr. Cantor was not interested in saving money, but he was fascinated with my dad's insistence on helping him. I was surprised and delighted at how quickly the two of them became great friends. I was stunned when we all got to the tailor shop in the backyard and both my dad and Mr. Cantor insisted I stay in the room with them. Finally, I realized that my dad had told Mr. Cantor that I had written scripts for my high school and junior college theatrical productions. They eventually asked me to leave the room, but I found out later that my dad had shown Mr. Cantor a couple of my scripts and that Mr. Cantor had told him that I should be writing professionally. In addition, he told my dad that if he would bring me to Hollywood, he would guarantee me some writing assignments in the entertainment industry.

When I got home from school that day, I saw two of my mother's big suitcases, and she had packed a lot of my clothes in them. My father then told me that Mr. Cantor thought it would be a great idea for me to come to Los Angeles. My father convinced Mr. Cantor to get me a job immediately. The most amazing thing is that he had also convinced my mother that I deserved a job, and the future looked great for me. He then convinced all of us that I should drive an old Plymouth (which Dad had just purchased for me). Then, Dad slipped a piece of paper in my pocket—Eddie Cantor's phone number—and said that I should call him the moment I got to LA.

After a lot of hard work and introductions in Los Angeles, I eventually met Dick Powell, who showed me all of the old scripts my father had sent him to read. Before I left Mr. Powell's office, he hired me to join the writing staff of his Four Star Television company. I can thank my dad for helping me with my dreams and making them come true. I just hope that Tori (my daughter) and Randy (my son) have received a portion of the dedication that my dad gave to me.

George M. Steinbrenner III

George M. Steinbrenner III is best known as the primary owner of the New York Yankees. Since he purchased the team in 1973, they have won ten pennants and six World Series titles. He is also known for his frequent appearances and caricatures in television and feature films, including the hit sitcom Seinfeld *and the Hollywood comedy* The Scout.

My father was an incredible man. He was highly intelligent (he graduated from MIT), a spectacular athlete (he was a champion hurdler), a successful businessman (at American Shipbuilding), and, most important, a loving husband and father. To this day, he remains the man I would want to have in a foxhole with me.

Here are just some of the many things he taught me:

- Always surround yourself with men who are smarter than you are.
- Always look to those who would criticize you rather than praise you—it is from your critics that you will learn the most.
- The speed of the leader determines the rate of the pack.
- You can't lead the cavalry if you can't sit in the saddle.
- Assume nothing!
- Trying is a poor third to doing.

Curtis Strange

A two-time U.S. Open champion golfer, Curtis Strange won consecutive national championships in 1988 and 1989, both on Father's Day. Curtis's father, Tom, died at age thirty-eight, when Curtis was fourteen.

I was so young when my father died—so it's tough. He taught me the game and brought me to the game of golf and the game of golf became my life. We didn't have talks about "life," but because my living is golf, I think of him every day.

We were both in the golf business, but in very different ways. I play golf for a living, but as a club professional, he served the public every day. He was the epitome of the old-fashioned country-club professional in that he taught people, drank beer with the members, and played gin with them. He liked to be around people and was very well liked. I attended the ceremony when my father was inducted into the Mid-Atlantic PGA Hall of Fame—the stories about him were flying that night.

I hear he was very tough and competitive when he did play, and I'd like to think I've inherited some of that tenacity. It's tough for me to socialize when I'm on the golf course. I don't mean it as an excuse, but I'm not gregarious. I would, however, like to live my life in such a way that I could be as well liked as he was.

Marlo Thomas

An actress, an activist, and the bestselling author of Free to Be You and Me, Free to Be a Family, Right Words at the Right Time, *and* Thanks and Giving All Year Long, *Marlo Thomas is the recipient of four Emmys and the Peabody Award, and is a Broadcasting Hall of Fame inductee. She serves as the National Outreach Director for St. Jude Children's Research Hospital and lives in New York with her husband, Phil Donahue.*

My father didn't have a lot of angst. That's unusual for a comedian. Most of the time, the best comedy writers and performers have a darker side that inspires their work. Woody Allen. Richard Pryor. Even Charlie Chaplin. Somehow, they manage to convert their anxiety into laughs. That's what makes them so funny.

But not my father. He was a naturally funny man; and while he wasn't what I'd call sunny, he didn't carry around a lot of baggage, or walk around with a cloud hanging over his head. His outlook on life was "live and let live," which made him one of the most unbigoted people I've ever known. He never insisted that anyone think the same way he thought, or be like him in any way. That's why all of his children felt unconditional love from him. He sent a message that said *You're okay,* and he had that down to an art. (My mother, on the other hand, was entirely different. If you didn't think precisely like she did, she took it as a personal insult!)

I remember once when my sister, Terre, and I were teenagers, we had taken a disliking to a so-called friend of our father's. As always, Dad had been very generous with this fellow—given him a career boost—but when my father needed a favor in return, the guy didn't deliver. He'd even been petty about it. But my father took it all in stride.

This didn't sit well with Terre and me.

"How can you be nice to that man?" Terre asked incredulously.

"You've been so generous to him," I added, "and he's not being generous back. Why would you ever want to give him the time of day again?"

My father turned to us, straightened up to his full height, and said, "I do not hunch my back with yesterday."

Over the years, I took my father's philosophy—just as I did with so many of the things he told me—and made it my own. I came to realize that holding a grudge is enormously unproductive. It doesn't change the person you're angry with one bit (in fact, that person usually doesn't even know you're upset with him or her), but it changes *you*. It makes you *heavier*. It gives you more to lug around.

Not hunching your back with yesterday speaks

about forgiveness. It speaks about moving on. And to me, it speaks directly to my father's giant heart.

After my father died in 1991, I received calls and letters from countless friends, expressing their sympathy. Everyone knew how deeply I loved my dad, and how much I would miss him. One of those letters came from a man with whom, years before, I'd had a falling out over a business deal in which I felt he had acted in bad faith. We hadn't spoken since.

"I know I'm probably not the person you want to hear from right now," his letter began, "but I thought I'd write anyway to tell you how sorry I am about the loss of your father. I know he meant the world to you, and I just wanted to let you know that you are in my thoughts."

I was touched by the letter, and wrote the man back, thanking him for his kindness. Because he'd mentioned our disagreement in his note, I acknowledged it in mine:

"I am my father's daughter," I wrote. "And like him, I do not hunch my back with yesterday . . ."

Alex Trebek

For more than twenty years, Alex Trebek has been the host of the hit game show Jeopardy! *He began his broadcasting career working in television and radio for the Canadian*

*Broadcasting Corporation, and has since received two
Emmy Awards and a star on the Hollywood Walk of Fame.*

My father, George Edward Trebek, immigrated to Canada from the Ukraine as a young teenager around the time of the Russian Revolution. He was on a train bound for farmwork near Winnipeg, Manitoba, but jumped off in Sudbury, Ontario, where he went on to spend most of his life working as a hotel chef. So much for farmwork.

He never received a formal education, and in fact never managed to lose his eastern European accent, but it was never a problem, even in a city like Sudbury, which was half English-speaking and half French. My dad had something far more valuable than book learning. He had a desire to work hard to better himself and the ability to see the good in everyone he met. As a result, he made a lot of friends, and in my entire life, I never encountered or heard of one enemy of his.

By example, he taught me the value of a kind heart, a generous soul, and unconditional love. Although he's been gone twenty-five years, I am still working on those lessons.

Donald Trump

One of the most famous American business executives of all time, Donald Trump is best known for his real-estate developments in Manhattan, where he owns several skyscrapers. He also owns several large casinos in Atlantic City. He has become one of television's most popular celebrities, serving as executive producer and star of The Apprentice.

I learned the best lessons about life from my father by example. He set high standards for himself, and he lived them every day. He was a 24/7 type of person when it came to integrity. That applied to both his personal life and his professional life, and it never wavered. Ever. He was steadfast to the very end, and he never pontificated about anything. Just watching him and being around him was the greatest lesson any person could have.

Admiral Stansfield Turner

A graduate of the United States Naval Academy and a recipient of a Rhodes scholarship to Oxford University, Admiral Stansfield Turner was appointed director of the Central Intelligence Agency by President Jimmy Carter in 1977 and served until 1981. He is a writer, a lecturer, and a regular television commentator.

At age eight, my father was an immigrant from England. At age fifteen, he had to quit high school after only two years in order to go to work to support his mother. Yet he educated himself and in time founded his own successful business. He taught me to have confidence that I could learn to do whatever I needed to do.

For instance, I decided I wanted to go to the U.S. Naval Academy. Father researched what I would need to do to get in. That included obtaining an appointment from a member of Congress, either a representative or a senator. Father, though, didn't have any political clout. He had not even voted for the representative from our district. He searched among his friends for those who had and importuned them to write Mr. Day on my behalf. Poor Mr. Day was inundated. Then Father sent me to Washington to call on Mr. Day—not once, but several times. Finally, the besieged congressman said to me, "Turner, I'll give you the next appointment I get." He knew that would not be for another year and probably assumed I'd give up by then.

Father also learned that a man in the next town had two boys in the academy, both of whom were football players. I had played football at a small college. Dad contacted this man, who contacted the assistant football coach at the academy. And Father sent me to Annapolis to see the coach twice. The second time was the same day the congressman had promised me his next appointment. Lo and behold, when I told that to the coach, he remembered that a midshipman who had been appointed by Mr. Day had just flunked out of the academy. Ipso facto, Mr. Day had an opening.

The next morning I walked into Mr. Day's office with this news and walked out with an appointment to Annapolis. The odds were almost insuperable when Father started this campaign for me. Studying all the requirements and diligently pursuing each of them beat those odds, however. The fact that Dad would work so hard to support me in this instance and many others meant so much to me. The fact that he showed me what thorough preparation and persistent effort could do has guided me in many, many instances in my life.

Ronan Tynan, M.D.

A founding member of the Irish Tenors, Dr. Ronan Tynan is perhaps most famous for his renditions of "God Bless America" performed during baseball games at Yankee Stadium. He has also amassed eighteen gold medals and fourteen world records in the Paralympic Games. In 2004, he left the Irish Tenors to pursue a solo career.

M y father was five feet four inches in stature, but even at that he was a giant of a man. I was born with a congenital deformity of my lower limbs in 1960, which was a difficult period in Ireland. But Dad was very strong and encouraged me and believed in me while he was alive.

When I was a small child, he would hug me and say I was great. When words are said with such sincerity and love you really believe them; you see in yourself what other people see in you—a strength waiting to be harvested.

He rejoiced in every success of my life. He was the match that lit the candle of my dreams.

I can still see his face the day I took my first step. It was as if the heavens had opened and given him the greatest gift. He was a very, very special man.

Dick Vitale

Dick Vitale coached high school, collegiate, and profes-sional basketball before joining ESPN in 1979, where he is a highly successful broadcaster and analyst. He is one of the definitive voices during the March Madness play-offs, where he is known for his spirited broadcasting style and extensive knowledge of NCAA basketball.

I pinch myself and thank God for allowing me to make a living doing something I absolutely love. When I think about how hard my mom and dad had to labor in order to provide for our family, it truly makes me appreciate how blessed I have been in my life.

I can't believe that I am paid handsomely to talk about a game that has captivated me for many, many years. Yes, college basketball has provided me with a life that has been like one big dream. As a basketball junkie, I get to sit courtside for ESPN covering the biggest matchups in the nation. For twenty-six years, I have been lucky to be behind the microphone calling major games such as Duke versus North Carolina. You get the picture—I am sixty-six years old, and I have a job that enables me to act like a kid.

It all started years and years ago growing up in Elmwood Park, New Jersey, which is located about twenty minutes from the George Washington Bridge in Bergen County. Man, what a house I had . . . it was filled with love, love, love. My dad was uneducated, but he had a doctorate in love. He never stopped teaching me numerous valuable lessons in how to succeed in the game of life. My dad working in a factory from 7 a.m. to 4 p.m. every day pressing coats—piecework, baby! The more ladies' coats he pressed, the more cash he made. My mom, despite having suffered numerous illnesses, including tuberculosis and later on a stroke, would drag her leg up and down the stairs to our cellar, where she would sew coats that my dad brought home. She would then proceed to make the greatest Italian meals that anyone could ever have. When dinner was over, my dad would go to his second job—he would put on a security guard uniform and work at the mall from 6 p.m. to 12 a.m.

Believe me, I learned more at my dinner table than in any class I ever took while earning my master's degree in education. I learned about love, family, the work ethic, loyalty, and all of the characteristics that helped to mold me in pursuing my goals. The inspiration I gained from my dad assisted me in becoming a scholastic, collegiate, and NBA coach.

My mom and dad were a valuable support tandem. It was a great feeling knowing that I could always rely on my dad for support and guidance. I can remember vividly coming home as a young high school coach and being totally depressed. All of my buddies would tell me that I would be teaching the sixth grade and coaching in high school my entire life. I would respond, "You may be right, but I am going to be the best sixth-grade teacher and coach I can possibly be." My friends told me to forget this crazy dream as I was not a big enough name, nor was I a former star player. My mom and dad would spot my sadness and would simply say, "Son, forget about what those people are saying, and don't ever, ever believe in the word 'can't.' " I would then hear the magical words that would fire me up when they said, "You are going to be somebody someday because you have spirit, Richie. [Richie is what my parents called me.] You have energy and enthusiasm and they can't take that away from you."

Let me tell you, it was always great to know that my dad thought I was the best. In fact, when I was fired by the NBA Detroit Pistons on November 8, 1979, I immediately called my mom and dad in Jersey. I wanted them to hear it from me first, rather than on the news. When I told them, my dad began to shout, "Are they crazy? Do they know what they are doing? Do they know how good you are?" My father would have you believing that I was better than the Wizard of Westwood, John Wooden, or Mr. NBA, Red Auerbach, or even "the General," Robert Montgomery Knight. Obviously, that is not valid, but it was always a great feeling to know that Dad was always my number one fan.

I will always remember October 20, 1997, as that was the day my dad succumbed to a variety of illnesses at the age of eighty-five. I told a crowd gathered at the Conte Funeral Home in Elmwood Park, New Jersey, as I eulogized him why my dad was the best man I ever met. His work ethic and his love for his family were so unique. And yes, my friends, I have been the beneficiary of having had a mom and dad who provided me with the greatest gift of all—unconditional *love*.

Mort Walker

Cartoonist Mort Walker is the author of the popular comic strips Hi and Lois *and* Beetle Bailey. *His other cartoons include* Boner's Ark *and* Sam & Silo *(with Jerry Dumas). He founded the Museum of Cartoon Art in 1974 and was inducted into the Museum of Cartoon Art Hall of Fame in 1989.*

While my dad was a well-known architect in the Midwest, a fine artist, an inventor, the poet laureate of Kansas, the president of the Missouri Writers Guild, and an accomplished pianist, he lacked one thing—financial success. He worked his tail off but never seemed to have any money. When I was a teenager and had a job, he used to borrow money from me. He went over budget building a church and lost our house. We had to go live with a friend.

Don't get me wrong. We loved our father. He was a wonderful man, fun to be with, an inspiration to many and a friend to all. He invented the first (and only) indoor miniature golf course but neglected to take into account that nobody during the Depression had a dime to play it. He invented a machine to cut pumice stone into building blocks and built one of our homes with them. The pumice stone was porous, collected moisture, and produced moss and mildew all over our walls. We moved.

But his big passion was baldness. He spent count-less hours, days, and years testing new "cures," saying that anyone who could grow hair on a bald head would make millions.

I was first aware of his experiments when I heard strange noises coming from our bathroom after I was in bed. He was using a plumber's plunger on his bald pate, hoping that it would suck the hair out. He gath-ered big green prickly hedge apples from the roadside and cooked them into a paste for his head, saying, "God put hedge apples on earth for some reason; maybe it was to cure baldness."

He went to the Kansas City stockyards to get newly slaughtered calves' bladders and put them on his head. His theory was that as the bladders dried up, they would pull the scalp together and allow the hair to come out. My mother's theory was that she wouldn't go out of the house with him until the hair made its appearance.

Abandoning the calves' bladders, he thought rub-ber cement might do the same job. He had a glass full of rubber cement that had hardened. He took it to the kitchen to heat it up so that he could spread it on his head. It exploded, and he staggered out of the kitchen, bleeding from the shattered glass. My mother summed it all up. "That's it!" she said.

Now what did I learn from my father, you're ask-ing? Well, I learned not to pursue "hair-brained" ideas unless you give them a better brain scan. I also vowed to save a percentage of everything I earned for a rainy day, and then never go out in the rain. As a result, I've always had money in the bank and hair on my head.

Brian Williams

Since joining NBC News in 1993, Brian Williams has become one of the nation's most accomplished and acclaimed anchors and traveling correspondents. He succeeded Tom Brokaw in the anchor chair on NBC Nightly News *effective December 1, 2004. He has been awarded three Emmys.*

My dad was a very taciturn New Englander, a physics major, and a World War II veteran. He was a quiet guy, and the term that I have always used to describe him is "good provider," in the truly best sense of the term. He is thoroughly a New Englander, however. I would say that the lesson I have learned from him chiefly is how to provide for your family without complaint. He is an anachronism in today's atmosphere of self-obsession and self-celebration. Because of age-based layoffs where he was working as an executive, he lost his job at age fifty. And we never knew then, but learned years later that our family came, evidently, within a few hundred dollars of having no money. But he would have none of it. He would do whatever he had to do to put food on the table and clothes on our backs, and it was crucial to him that we never find out. We were never allowed to see him sweat. He never complained a day in his life about getting on the 6:10 a.m. train to go into the city and coming home after dark with a briefcase full of work.

It was a different age—and, by the way, I think we could use a little bit of that today, when every word, every motion, every exertion is now discussed in our current society. Only the individual is celebrated, that kind of thing. He is a product of another age. I think in many ways that it might have been a better age. His work ethic is his living legacy. To this day, while I am the most fortunate person I know, and while I am able to say that I am doing what I dreamed of doing as a child, if it all came apart, if it all fell to pieces tomorrow, I feel it in my DNA that I could do whatever I had to do for a living—two jobs, three jobs, shift work, work nights—to provide for my family. So that actually gives me confidence in my life. I'm not wedded to what I do to the extent that I would lose my identity if I lost my ability to pursue my occupation through an accident or wrongdoing or some other reason. I am very confident, because I have done a lot of jobs in my life. I've spent many years without money, many years without health insurance. I am very confident in my own ability to look out for my family and provide for our needs.

Al Yankovic

"Weird" Al Yankovic is a musician and a humorist known for his hilarious parodies of popular songs. During his Grammy Award–winning career, he has had four gold and four platinum records. He is also a successful music video director.

My father was not a career-obsessed man—he had simple tastes, he made a modest living, and that was perfectly fine with him. He never measured success by material possessions or power. He always told me that a man was successful if somehow he was lucky enough to make a living by doing something he loved. And while my father was still with us, I know he took great pride in my career achievements—but I think he was happiest in knowing that I was able to make a living by doing something that made *me* happy. That's probably the greatest lesson he ever taught me.

Well, that, and the thing about watermelon. He taught me that watermelon is the Happy Fruit. He always used to tell me, "Son, if you're ever suicidally depressed or at the end of your rope, just go out and find a nice ripe watermelon, then throw it down on the floor and cram as much of it in your mouth as you possibly can. It'll cheer you right up."

And you know what? It does.

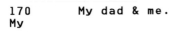